The l

of a

Turpentine Girl

Sarah Evelyn Holland Shaw

ISBN 978-1-64258-500-1 (paperback)
ISBN 978-1-64258-501-8 (digital)

Christian Faith Publishing, Inc.
832 Park Avenue
Meadville, PA 16335
www.christianfaithpublishing.com

Printed in the United States of America

Table of Contents

Acknowledgement

I have been writing my story for four years. I could not have shared my story without my family and these two very special people. I would like to dedicate my book to Jill, my daughter, and Hollie Bullard, a technology training technician.

God sent many special angels when I needed them the most. Jill encouraged me to keep writing week after week. She helped me with every page of this book. She took me to all the places that you will read about in this book.

Hollie typed and re-typed day and night to preserve it. She put in many hours to help put my story into the written word.

I would like to thank my daughter, Tammy, for helping me while Jill worked on the book.

Thank you to Joan Wilson, Carol Welch and Brookie Connell who spent many hours editing each page of my book.

I sincerely love and appreciate all of my special angels.

A special thanks to Joyce Kramer. Ms. Kramer writes for the *Post-Searchlight*. She wrote a series of articles on turpentine stills. Her articles were very helpful in the explanation of the process of making turpentine.

My thanks to the Georgia Museum of Agriculture and Historic Village and their staff, especially Levi Alvarado and Ms. Cosper. The Historic Village and Museum helped secure information and photos for my book.

Most important, I thank God for allowing me to live long enough to share my story.

Sarah Evelyn Holland Shaw
Bainbridge, Georgia
February 2016

Prologue

The Turpentine Girl

From Left to Right: Lottie, Wilford, and
Evelyn. In the Chair: James

I was born close to Pearson, Georgia. Oh, you have never heard of it? Well, it's about three miles from Willacoochee, Georgia. Oh . . . you don't know where that is either? Well, let me see if I can describe it better. Have you heard of Tifton, Georgia? Pearson is several miles on the other side of Tifton going toward Waycross, Georgia. Oh, you know where that is, well, okay then.

Ten miles from Pearson, Georgia, I came into this world on February 4, 1923. My dad was the manager of a turpentine still. He loved to work with a group of black men and work with pine trees.

The pine trees in those days were used to extract pine sap for various uses. We do not have that same process today, but while I was growing up, I lived and enjoyed ten turpentine stills in my life.

As I was growing up, I knew that my dad was a very sweet man and would give you the shirt off his back. However, he did have a problem. My dad liked his home brew. He was seven years older than my mother. She married him very quickly. I don't think she knew how much he loved his home brew.

My dad could sing really well. Sometime after the first three children were born and on some weekends when he was home and in a good mood, he would sit on the front porch and sing, and it was so much fun. In my heart, I believed I was his favorite child. What brought me to that thought was sometimes Wilford and Lottie, my brother and sister, would gang up on me. (I was the middle child). When Dad caught wind of it and decided we needed whipping, he did not whip me as hard. One day, after we finished singing, Daddy said something to my mother. They started fussing. Mama went to the kitchen and came back with a frying pan and hit him with it! Afterwards, that was the last of the fussing. For the rest of my life, I never saw that again.

Sometimes, when Daddy came home and he had had a bad day, Mama would say, "You kids go to your room and stay there. I'll tell you when to come out." Mama would feed Daddy and put him to bed, and he would sleep it off and go back to work the next day. Daddy had a very hard job. He had to keep track of all the trees that were chipped each day. He had a counting machine that he kept in his hand all day and it would count for him. I know many people knew nothing about a turpentine still. An excellent description of this process was listed in our local paper by Joyce Kramer. I am including this information so you will have an idea about the business of turpentine stills.

Turpentine Still Processing The Value of a Turpentine Still

In America, the main source of turpentine is the long-leaf pine tree and the slash pine tree. The extraction of this sticky liquid, turpentine, is the basis for many products.

Long ago, it was used in oil lamps, soap, ink, as well as medicine for astringents and drugs for destroying intestinal parasites such as tapeworms. Baseball players and musicians used a byproduct, resin, for a better grip on the bat and to keep the violin bow from sticking. Turpentine resin is even mentioned in the Bible: "God told Noah to build an ark. He told Noah to pitch his ark with resin within and without to make it sea worthy."

Getting the Resin

The crude gummy substance called resin was obtained from living pine trees by cutting the bark in strips.

The most popular way to get sap from the tree was to use a cup that was made from tin and hung from a nail on the tree. First, a cut was made in the tree close to the ground.

The bark was peeled off to make that part of the tree flat. Then a twelve-inch piece of tin was nailed to the tree with a single nail.

It was bent on the sides to look like a gutter. Then the cup was attached to the tree. The shape of the cup was about six inches wide and twelve to fifteen inches long. This was placed under the lower part of the metal strip. It was held in place with a tin penny nail.

The next step was to carve a perfect *V* in the bark. The tree was scoured upward in a widening *V*. The pulley was taken to pull back the bark. It was first pulled on one side of the *V* and then on the other. Dippers would come by every ten days or so and empty the cups. That is where my daddy took over. He was a manager and a wood rider. He had to count every box that was emptied. He only worked with the black people that lived around the still. He also had to keep account of the chippers.

Vivian as Wood Rider

Vivian - Pictured Above

The chippers carried a small nail keg with a handle.

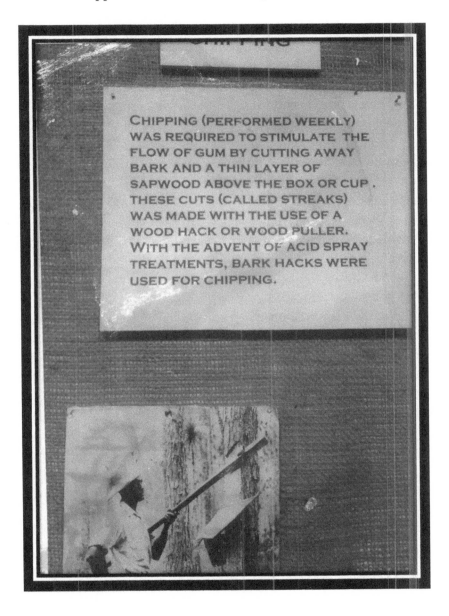

They would pour waste of the contents in the cup. A flat-shaped tool was used to go into the cup and scoop out the collected resin. The resin was placed in kegs, and from there it was poured into barrels which were then hauled out of the woods to the still. The still was housed in an open two-story structure with a kettle resting on a fireplace.

The raw sap was placed in a large kettle to cook. It had a metal spout on one side which went over into an open vat. The sap was then strained three times. The first time, it went through a metal screen and the impurities gathered on the screen. The second and third times, it was strained through cotton batting. This removed all the needles and bark and other trash from the sap. The sap was then placed in metal drums and wooden barrels. The drums and barrels were made right there at the still. Once they were full, they took the barrels to Pensacola, Florida.

Most all of the stills were alike, and when they strained the resin and put it up to cool, my brother and sister and I would take the trash after it was drained and make balls to play with. They were hard but we had fun with them. At Christmas time, we had some kind of tree that had a cluster of balls the size of tennis balls. Mother would get bunches of the balls from the tree and dip them in the hot resin. When the balls were dry, they were so pretty. We used this to decorate all over the house at Christmas. The balls would shine like crystal.

Turpentine Commissary

Every still that we lived at had a commissary, and Daddy ran the commissary. Every Saturday, he would pay the hired hands, and off they would go to buy their groceries. Daddy would deduct their groceries from their paycheck.

We also lived out of the commissary. We did have some canned meat. It was called tripe in a can.

It was tough no matter how it was cooked. All we could do was suck on it and spit it out. We were only allowed so much for food. Mama had to make it last for three children and her and Daddy. Because of this, my mother was going without to make sure everyone else was fed, and she became very sick. Mama developed pellagra. This was a sickness due to not having enough to eat. I remember a lot of times we had syrup and hoecakes, which was flour or cornmeal and water mixed together to make the hoecake.

I guess that was during the recession because it wasn't that way all the time. When I was young, way back in the twenties, I believed all of life would be like one perfect summer day. After all, it did start that way. There isn't much I can say about our earliest childhood except that it was very good, and for that, I should be grateful. We were not the richest and we were not the poorest. If we lacked any necessities, I couldn't name them. If we had luxuries, I couldn't name them either. We were just run-of-the-mill children. Of all the places that we lived, no one seemed to have more or less than our family. We knew we were loved, and that is what seemed to be the most important thing anyway. We had some good times together, and I want to share those good times with you.

Chapter 1

The Life of a Turpentine Girl: Sarah Evelyn Holland Shaw

My grandfather was William Dodson Kilgore. He lived in the country about two miles from Mystic, Georgia. (Number 1 on map) He had a large farm and farmhouse located on a tremendous hill. It wasn't fancy, but it was home.

William Dodson Kilgore

The house had a great big hall down the middle. The bedrooms were on each side, and at the end of the hall was a breezeway. That was the coolest place anywhere. Many summers we would go and visit my grandparents, and I recall that my brothers and sister and I would come in for lunch after working and take an hour nap in that breezeway. The kitchen was built on the back of the breezeway, and that was where the good food was. After eating a good, hearty lunch, we would head back to the cotton patch.

My grandmother, Sarah Dryden Kilgore

William and Sarah and Their Children
Left to Right: Mae Bell, William, and Mary

My grandmother and grandfather had four boys and three girls. My mother, Mae Bell Kilgore Holland Greenwood, was the oldest girl and the second child. When she was sixteen years old, her mother died. My mother was absolutely lost. Since my mother was the oldest girl, she had to assume the duties of motherhood. These duties were cooking, washing clothes, and taking care of all the younger children. She did not mind, but it seemed to be too much for a sixteen-year-old. Of course, all her brothers and sisters helped out when they were not working in the fields. For years, I listened as my mother told me tales of how her working days would be.

Mae Bell as a
Younger Child

Mae Bell's Class Picture

Chapter 2

My Mother
Mae Bell Holland's
Working Days

My mother had long work days every single day. Monday was always wash day. Mama had to get water from the well to fill two wash tubs. One tub was used for the wash water and the other was the rinse water.

She started with a wash pot, pouring water into it. She built a fire under this pot using fat wood chips from our woodbox.

She put homemade soap in the water and stirred to mix it up good. She then filled the pot with the clothes that were the dirtiest and boiled them good. Using an axe handle, she moved the clothes out of the pot into the washtub. She then took a rubboard and scrubbed the clothes up and down until the clothes were clean.

The Rubboard

At that time, the clothes were moved into the rinse water. She rinsed and rinsed and then had to squeeze each piece of clothing to get the water out. Now it was time to hang them up to dry. She had a clothes pin bag, so up and down she went, hanging the clothes. After the clothes were dry, she would fold what she could and save the rest for ironing.

The next day was ironing day. She had two ole hand irons that had to be heated on the wood stove or over the fireplace. She would sit the iron in front of the fire and let it get red hot. She would take one iron and wipe the flat side with a rag so as not to dirty the clothes. She started with one iron and used it until the iron cooled off. Then she would swap to the other iron. That went on all day until she was through. Monday and Tuesday were spent washing and ironing. During these two days, she still had to find time for cooking, making beds, washing dishes, and anything else that had to be done. Mama had to heat the irons in summer and winter. That had to be hard to do on a hot summer day.

I can only imagine the life my mother had in her teenage years. She told me she had worked and worked and had about enough of it.

Bedroom with bed made daily, small desk with ole timey
wooden chair, wooden floors, and ole timey slop jar

A slop jar was customary back during those days. Every household had one underneath the bed. Custom had it that women didn't
go out to the outhouse at night. Every morning, the slop jars were
taken out to the outhouse, emptied, washed, and put back under
the bed. Old newspapers were put under and around them, and the
newspapers had to be taken out and burned.

Chapter 3

Mae Bell's Proposal

Mae Bell and Vivian Holland

One day, while Mama was tending to daily chores, she saw a small boy walking down the road toward the house. He was looking for her to give her a note from his brother.

The note read, "Miss Mae Bell, will you marry me?"

She told me that she didn't know this person very well. She had seen him a few times and knew that he lived down the road. She said,

"I knew he was cute, and I wanted to get out of this housework I was having to do."

So she quickly wrote back on a note: "Yes, I will marry you. When?"

In a few days, Mae Bell left home with her husband-to-be, Vivian Holland.

Chapter 4

Waldo Henderson's Still
Sarah Evelyn Holland's
Birth and Early Childhood

At the age of sixteen, my mother married Vivian Holland at the courthouse in Irwinville, Georgia. They moved to Lax, Georgia, to live. (See map number 2). They lived in Lax about a year when along came their first child, Wilford Dotson Holland. He was born November 2, 1920. I do know that during their time in Lax, my mother lost a son, and I also know she never talked about it very much. My parents did not stay in Lax very long. They moved out in the country near Pearson, Georgia, (see map number 3) to Waldo Henderson Turpentine Still.

At this location was a huge home, and in the back of the home was a smaller home. This small home was the birthplace of Sarah Evelyn Holland.

Fireplace of house where Sarah Evelyn Holland was born.

A tree still stands at the old home place near Pearson, Georgia. I entered this world on February 4, 1923. I was delivered by a midwife. Mother never had a doctor.

My brother Wilford was three years older than I was. We slept in a big room with a fireplace. We would lie there and listen as our parents talked every night. We were all ears until we drifted off to sleep. When I was one and one half years old, along came a baby sister, Miss Lottie Mae Holland.

It seemed as if she grew up in a hurry because I remember quite well Lottie running around the house playing with Wilford and me. I have a very distinct memory that one day, she got mad at Wilford and threw a brick at him. It missed him and hit me squarely in the head. I was bleeding like a stuffed pig, and I had a big knot on my head. I remember Mama stopped the bleeding by placing spiderwebs right smack on the spot where I was bleeding. The spot was okay, but Miss Lottie Mae was not. I won't tell you what happened to her.

The house we lived in was very small. It had a big room with a fireplace, a bedroom, and a kitchen. It had a small room off to the side that was forbidden for us to go in. Of course, that made us very curious. Wilford dared me to look in there. I told him to look since he was the oldest. Well, of course, you know who poked their head in the room. Yes, Miss Lottie Mae.

We asked her, "What's in the room?"

She said, "She didn't see anything but a big washtub sitting in the middle of the floor with some stinky stuff in it."

We found out from Mama that our daddy was making home brew, that is something like beer. Daddy didn't want us to know.

Mama had a beautiful lamp she bought from a traveling salesman. She asked us not to touch it. It was really the only thing in the house worth having. It was so pretty. It looked like a Tiffany lamp. The lamp was sitting on a newspaper, and Miss Lottie Mae decided she wanted the newspaper. Well, you guessed it! There went the lamp, and, of course I can't tell you what happened to Miss Lottie Mae. You would think she could learn her lesson by now.

The Paramore family lived in a big white house across the road from our house. Ms. Paramore was my teacher. I was five years old and was in premier which is the same as kindergarten now. Ms. Paramore took Wilford and me to school every day. The school was a one-room school house that had a potbelly stove right in the middle of it. It was our source of heat and kept us very warm.

Ms. Paramore taught all the grades. She taught me how to read, and I remember my first book was called *Little Baby Ray*.

I loved it. At school, we had an outside bathroom. One day, it was pouring down rain and a group of girls had to go to the bathroom. We crowded together under an umbrella and started down the path to the outhouse bathroom. The next thing you know, I got pushed down in the mud. I had mud all over my homemade panties, and all the girls were just laughing at me. I was one more muddy mess.

The girls never lifted a finger to help me out of the mud. They did beat a path to tell the teacher that I fell in the mud. My teacher made the ordeal a million times worse. She took me inside and took my homemade flour-sack panties off and took me outside to the water pump and turned my little butt up to wash the mud off. Of course, she did this in front of the entire class. I was so embarrassed. She washed my panties out and hung them by the stove to dry. All the kids in the class knew I was sitting there all day without any panties on. They would snicker and laugh at me. For some strange reason, my parents just happened to pick me up early from school that day. We were going to my grandparents. I've never been so glad to leave a schoolroom in my life.

Mama just happened to have an extra pair of panties in the car. I guess as long as I live, I will never forget the most embarrassing school day of my life.

Chapter 5

The Move Across the Road
In the Big White House

One day, my daddy came home and told us we were going to move into the big white house across the road that had belonged to the Paramores. They were moving to Ocilla, Georgia. That was a happy day for me because I had loved that house for as long as I could remember. The house had a long porch all across the front. There was a bedroom for each of the kids. It had a long hall down the middle, and we had a cool place to play. There was a big pasture outside the house with a wooden fence between it and the house. We liked that because we could walk on it.

There was a large, and I do mean *large*, oak tree at the end of the pasture and a hull of an old building that we could play in when it rained. Wilford, Lottie, and I could climb to the very top of that old oak tree.

My daddy had the only radio in the neighborhood. He would invite everybody to our house on Saturday night to hear the Grand Ole Opry or a boxing match. Everybody came with their children, and all of us played until we became sleepy. Mama would spread quilts and make pallets on the floor for all the children. We would sleep until the radio went off about midnight. When the radio would go off, Mama would wake us up and say, "Guess what we have?"

Bologna Sandwiches

 and

Watermelon

Daddy's boss man had a croquet set and all his friends played with it. It looked like fun. We knew we couldn't afford one, so we looked in the Sears and Roebuck Catalogue and saw what they looked like. We knew then what we had to do to make it. We cut up part of Mama's clothesline to make the wickets. We cut limbs off the chinaberry tree to make the mallets. We would get hot tar from the turpentine still and got the stuff that was strained from the liquid turpentine and made our balls. We had our own croquet set and we played with it a very long time. Of course, we didn't make it overnight. It took us a long time, but nevertheless we did it.

My sister and I were very close in age. We were only one and half years apart. We did everything together. We cut out the girls and dresses out of the Sears and Roebuck Catalogue. We played paper dolls with these. We would paste the dresses on with flour and water. They would stay on the paper doll for a while. We cut out pictures of furniture, ice box refrigerators, and most anything we could find in the book. We would make us a big playhouse with all those things. That was a good project on a rainy day when we had to play inside.

Every year, we had a big, fat salesman come by selling some kind of salve for the community and he had to spend the night with us. He always brought a bunch of paperback books and color crayons for us children. We looked forward to seeing him, but Mama didn't. He would eat meals with us, and he would eat everything in sight. Many times, there was nothing left for us kids to eat. Mama was glad to see him go.

Someone had given Mama some pecans and that was a luxury for us. She hid them under the bed and told us not to bother the pecans. She was going to use them for cooking at Christmas. Well, while Mother was taking a nap, three sets of hands grabbed some pecans and headed to the shed for a yummy good time. I was sitting up on a shelf eating mine, and one of them dropped out of my hand and hit the ground and before I could jump down and get it, Wilford saw it and started racing after it and caused me to fall. I fell and hit my forehead on the steel rim of the barrel, and of course, I was bleeding like a stuffed pig again. We had to go and tell Mama.

After putting spiderwebs on my forehead to stop the bleeding, you can only imagine what she put on the other end of our bodies. We could get into some kind of trouble.

Pictured is the Singer Sewing Machine

My mother sewed for the public. She had us play outside while she worked. We would only come inside for lunch because everything else we needed was outside. Wilford, Lottie, and I were like the Three Stooges.

Evelyn, Wilford, and Lottie as children

We only had each other to play with. There were no neighbors there to play with. We had some kind of imagination growing up with our playthings. We made what we played with.

One day, Wilford said, "What are we going to do today?"

I said, "Let's make a car!"

Wilford said, "How do you do that?"

I showed him. I sent him to the house to get shovels, an axe, and a hammer. We started digging in the dirt. We had dug out a section between the seats and made a ridge so we could start a back seat.

Wilford said, "That looks good."

I had to find a stick to put in the front to hold the steering wheel. Then we had to find a lid from an old can somewhere to make a steering wheel. We did make it, and stood back and looked at our completed car.

Wilford said, "Let's go for a ride."

All three of us got in the car. Wilford drove and Lottie was in the front seat with him and I was in the back seat. We pretended we were going for a ride so off we would go singing, "I'm bound for the Promise Land."

Jump board pictured above

Lottie and I had a jump board. We would put a board across a log. She would get on one end and I would get on the other. She would jump on one end, sending me sailing through the air. I would come down and she would go sailing pretty high. It was so much fun unless you missed the board coming down; then it would take the skin off your shin. That's when we would holler for Mama and out came the spiderwebs to stop the bleeding. We decided at that point to leave the board alone for a while.

We never lacked for anything to do. We would walk that wooden fence, turn cartwheels, walk around the yard on our hands, and climb the ole oak tree to the top. Never once do I remember asking Mama, "What can we do?" We kept fully entertained all day long. We never had enough time to play with all the things we wanted to.

Lottie and I drew a play house in the dirt. We would make the house out of shoe boxes. We collected colored glass for our dishes in the kitchen. We also had bald-headed dolls. I told Lottie I wanted dolls with hair.

She said, "I want dolls with hair too, but what can we do about it?"

I said, "I bet if we stick a hole in the top of the dolls head and put some corn silk in it we can make the doll some hair."

We had a cornfield beside our house. In the field, we found blonde hair and some red hair. Well, what do you know, we had a doll with hair. I was so proud of them. Of course, you know it was a white-colored corn silk and a red-colored corn silk.

My mother not only sewed for the public, she would also make our clothes. She would have Lottie and me pick the dresses we wanted from the Sears and Roebuck Catalogue. She would order material and use a newspaper to cut out a pattern of the dresses we wanted. She would have a dress made by the time we got home from school. She was a good and fast seamstress. We were the best-dressed children in school.

We looked so good in our dresses, but underneath were our homemade panties. They were made out of flour sacks and one piece of elastic held together with a safety pin. Every time we changed our panties, we changed the elastic. We didn't dare lose our safety pin!

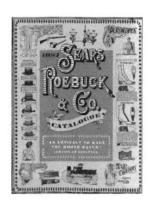

Chapter 6

Kirkland School:
Third Grade

Kirkland School as it is today

I was eight years old now and in the third grade. I went to Kirkland School. Our bus driver came to our house early in the morning. He ate breakfast with us every morning. He lived about ten miles away in Pearson, Georgia. Wilford and I were the first children to get on the bus in the morning. Lottie was too young to go to school. On a real cold day, Mama would bundle us up so much we could hardly move. She would give us hot sweet potatoes to put in our coat pockets to keep our hands warm. Then we would eat them for supper that night.

We did not have school buses like they do today. Our bus had flaps for curtains on the windows. The flaps were made with thick material, and it had a long stick which ran through a hole at the end and pulled all the way through. It was tied down at each end to keep it from flapping in the wind. It didn't keep all the cold wind out. It could get very cold. On our journey to and from school, which was about a ten-mile trip, we had to cross Pig Creek and Hog Creek. It was a one-way dirt road that got very boggy at times.

Most mornings we were on time, and some mornings we were stuck in Hog Creek. We spent half our school day stuck until someone came and pulled us out. If we didn't get stuck going to school, we would get stuck coming home at night. Mother just went ahead and packed lunch and supper so we would have something to eat.

It would usually be after dark before we got home. Most of the time, if we got stuck close to home, the bus driver would start blowing his horn, and Daddy would come get us out of the mud.

I remember before we ever started school, Daddy would take us to town to get some new school shoes. This is the only time we ever got to go to town. He would take us in the store and we had to get hi-top black tennis shoes. Daddy would make me and Wilford buck dance for the guy who waited on us before he would let us have our shoes. Don't you know that was very exciting for the clerk to see? Ha!

The days we actually made it to school, I really did enjoy it. Every recess, our teacher would send someone around to see if we wanted candy. You could get a one-penny sucker or anything you wanted as long as it only cost a penny. There was a little store next to the school, and we took advantage of it. Mama would give Wilford and me a penny most every day and that *was* something special!

Just as you have those special memories, you also have those not-so-special memories. Some that have a tendency to stick with you for a lifetime. One day, while I was at recess, I noticed a little girl sitting in a car with the door open and she was crying. I went over to her to ask if I could help her. I soon heard a voice shouting, "Get away from my little girl, you are ugly enough to make a bear cry!" It didn't take me long to get away. It was my teacher talking who was also the child's mother. I can still hear that voice as if it were yesterday.

Another thing I do remember about those days at school was that we had to study our lessons by a kerosene lamp or by firelight. I really don't see how we did what we did.

We didn't have grass yards and at our house we had wooden floors. Mama would scrub them with a homemade mop made out of corn shucks. We also had homemade brooms. We swept the floors and the yards. Mama made our rugs out of corn shucks, and we had some pretty ones.

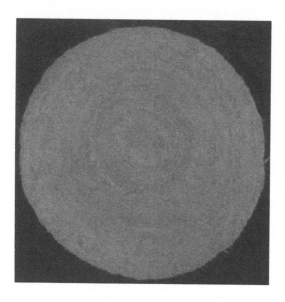

Chapter 7

Fun Times with My Family

One Sunday morning my daddy said, "Get your swimsuits ready. We are going to the beach at St. Simons Island. We are going to see *Old Iron Side*." Old Iron Side was a ship that was docked for years at St. Simons. Daddy liked to go and see it every year. Mama made a picnic lunch and we loaded up the car to go. There was always an extra group to join us. We would be three deep in the back seat of that car.

When we got to the beach, Daddy drove way down the beach so we would be isolated. The boys would swim in their short pants.

There were four girls, and we had to take turns with one swimsuit. I had to wait an hour before I could swim. We even had to share a turn with our visitors. We were having so much fun, we did not notice the tide had come in. Daddy could not take us off the beach the way he brought us on. He just turned the car and drove straight up the embankment. We were all scared to death, but he got us out of there safe and sound.

The third Sunday in July was always the day Daddy wanted to go to the singing convention in Mystic, Georgia (see map number 1). He gave us about a week to get ready. Mama ordered dresses from Sears and Roebuck for Lottie and me to wear. When they arrived, we had a blue organdy one and a yellow one with ruffles all the way down.

Lottie ended up with the beautiful blue one, and I was stuck with the yellow one. Lottie was beautiful and plump and had blonde hair. Mama thought the blue did her well. I was skinny and had mousy-brown hair, and I was stuck with the yellow one. (to this day I hate yellow) Off we went to the singing convention in our new dresses, and we itched and scratched in the rumble seat of our car and we itched and scratched as we played in them all day long.

Daddy would give us a nickel to spend at the ice-cream stand. We had all day to make up our minds if we wanted to buy candy or ice cream. We squeezed that nickel all day long, trying to decide. The ice cream won out every time.

Chapter 8

Summertime at Granddaddy's

Every summer, we would spend a week with our grandfather. We would stay there two days, and then walk about a mile down the road to a small shack. This house belonged to my Aunt Mary and Uncle Virgie. They had two children. My Uncle Virgie played the fiddle and all the kids would dance and sing. We would jump up and down on a mattress on the floor they had placed there for us to sleep on. It was in front of the fire to keep us warm. Their house didn't have windows, just flaps or shutters to fill in the hole in the walls. We didn't care. We had a great time. After spending two days there, we would walk to Uncle William and Aunt Erma's house. They had two children, Billy and Jimmy. Both are deceased now.

Their house was not a bit better, but that did not get in the way of our fun. Aunt Erma was about three hundred pounds and a jolly ole soul. Uncle William was tall and weighed about one hundred and fifty pounds. What a combination they were, but we loved it there.

Our next two days on our vacation were farther away, so Granddaddy would come and get us and drive us to Uncle Elbert and Aunt Beulah's house. They had two girls, Sarah and Lou Belle. We loved it there because all of us played together. We played dolls, hopscotch, jump rope, and hide-and-seek. Here again, it was just so much fun spending time with family.

We spent the rest of our summer with Granddaddy. Boy, did we have some experiences there! He let us pick cotton and work in tobacco. We also learned to shake out peanuts.

When I mentioned that I picked cotton, I made it sound like it was fun. I found out it is not fun. We started our day early in the morning dew.

Cotton Sack

I had a cotton sack big enough to hold one hundred pounds. It was made with a strap that went over your head to your shoulder. You picked the soft cotton out of the four section of a spur. It was very sharp on each prong. It was not easy to pick. You had to reach down and get the cotton and put it in your sack as fast you can. You wanted to fill the sack to one hundred pounds. It was very hard for me to do. We would get one dollar for every one hundred pounds we picked. My uncles would leave me way behind. While I was picking, my back and knees would hurt. I prayed every day it would rain and soak my cotton sack so my sack would weigh one hundred pounds. I think my uncles weighed it and told them I had one hundred pounds so as not to hurt my feelings. I did the best I could, but if I had to make a living picking cotton, I would starve to death. Cotton pickers should be happy that someone invented a real cotton picker. No more skint knees and hurt backs.

I would like to tell you that working in tobacco was better, but trust me, it was not. I know everybody has seen tobacco barns all over South Georgia. Did you ever wonder what went on in those barns?

I know the barns have outlived their use for tobacco now, but in our days on my grandfather's farm, this is what took place. I joined my two uncles in the rows of tobacco that had to be suckered. This was the start of the process before taking it to the market.

The tobacco stalk has a long stem in every plant. The stem had to be taken out of every plant. It was as slick as okra. When you did row after row of this, your hand got so sticky. I couldn't wait to wash my hands. After finishing with that patch of tobacco, we had to take the leaves off the stems and take them to the barn in bags that were placed in a wagon and pulled by a mule. As we did each row, the mule actually moved along with us.

In the tobacco barn, it had sticks about three feet long and string in place waiting for the tobacco. The workers would then take over. We worked at the barn. There was a rack and the sticks laid across from end to end of the rack. My job, using both hands, was to hand the tobacco to another worker. That worker would stand at the end of the stick and put the tobacco on both sides of the stick with a string holding it on. They did both sides at one time, and you had to be fast to do that.

Our job was to keep feeding these workers with the tobacco, and we had to be as fast as the other workers.

When the sticks were full, there was another worker there to pick it up and start placing them on the highest racks in the barn. This process went on all day until the barn was full. After the barn was full all the way to the top, they started a fire and timed it. It would take three days and nights to cook it or until the leaves turned brown. When the tobacco cooled off, it was taken out of the barn and taken off the sticks and placed in big bags. The bags were placed in a wagon and carried by mule to the house to be placed in the breezeway. It was our job to grade the tobacco. We had a best pile, a not-so-good pile, and a pile.

My Uncle George and Uncle Gordon were the supervisors in all the operations. When we finished the grading and our uncles checked it over, the tobacco was placed back in the bags either good hay or bad hay. After this, it was time for the tobacco to head to the market. It was fun to go to the market and see it auctioned off.

The way I described all this did not take place in a day. It was a big thing to do and most of the farmers would help each other so they wouldn't have to hire so many people. While one barn was cooking with a worker looking on, my grandfather and his other helpers would go to another neighbor's and help him get his tobacco to his barn.

The tobacco farms are not in business now since the government cracked down on smoking. Most of the barns you see now are getting old and just standing for people to look at. I know some people are remembering how good it was when you could see smoke coming out of the chimney.

My sister, brother, and I thought we were through with our work when we finished tobacco and cotton. We were ready for some fun things and to rest awhile. My grandfather had other ideas. He asked us if we were ready to do so more work. We just looked at each other, smiled, and said "Yes!"

We asked him, "What in the world is next?"

He said, "I thought you could help me shake some peanuts." He explained my uncle would plow up the peanuts and we would come up behind him and pick up each bundle and shake as much dirt as we could off the peanuts and then lay them back in a row.

ew in the Southern States. Much of the land is as level as
___ in this field is the peanut, which the boys and

We never heard of such a job, but you can believe we did what we were told to do. Early in the morning, we were in the peanut field, getting dirtier by the minute. It wasn't such a bad job. I just know we shook a lot of dirt in a day. My uncle had big bales out in another field, and he would come behind us as soon as we shook the dirt off, and he would pick the peanuts up with a peanut machine. He would take the peanuts to these poles and stack them all around the poles all the way to the top. Then we would pick the peanuts from the vine and sack them up. The peanuts were then taken to the market.

PEANUT HARVESTING—OLD AND NEW
Peanut combines such as the one on Dan
Bridges farm in Terrell County, below, i.
harvesting most of Georgia's peanuts. A few
years ago, most were hand-stacked as in the
field above. See the peanut combine parade
on Page 6. Additional tips on combining and
curing your crop on Pages 8B, 10B and 10D.

As you can see, we were always busy at Granddaddy's. We learned so much in those days, and since I'm now ninety-one years old, I look back over those days of working in tobacco, picking cotton, and shaking peanuts. I think what a great adventure for me and my sister and brother. I think to myself, *Children in this era of life will never have the chances that we did.*

The kids now do not even know that butter comes from a cow. They don't see the connection. They just eat butter and never think about it. This was another great chance I learned at Granddaddy's. He taught me to milk a cow. They didn't have ice back then, so when we milked the cow, we would put the milk in jars and had a special well to keep the milk in. We tied a long rope around the jar, and let the jar down in the well to keep it cold.

Cold Storage for Milk

We kept some of the milk out and let it set. The cream would settle to the top, and Aunt Mattie would take the cream and put it in a five-gallon churn. The churn had a dash and a long stick that looked like a broom handle but was not that long.

Butter Churn

My sister and I had the job of churning the milk. We took a hold of the stick that was in a lid with a hole in the top, and we would go up and down until the cream in that milk would turn to butter. Lottie and I had to take turns churning because our hands and arms would get so tired. After the butter was done, we would take it out of the churn and wash it off with water and put it in a mold or dish. It would be so pretty, yellow, and good. The milk left in the churn became buttermilk, and we would drink this with some good ole cornbread. *Yum, yum, good!*

Oh, all of our jobs at Granddaddy's paid off. He gave us five dollars for the work we had done. That was big money for us.

I saved mine to get a permanent in my hair and to buy socks for school. This is the way the permanent was given in those days: when I say "permanent," it was really different than it is today.

We were wired with a head full of rollers that were hooked up to electricity on the wall. It cooked for so many minutes, and then they were taken off. They combed it out, and I had enough curls to last my whole term of school. You certainly got your money's worth.

My Granddaddy Kilgore killed hogs and made sausage. It was really something to see. My Aunt Mattie, Granddaddy's second wife, would can the sausage in jars. I can tell you the time I spent on that farm in the summer was an experience I will always cherish.

At Granddaddy's house, they had a well in their front yard for drinking water. They had a gourd dipper that hung by the well, and everyone drank out of the gourd. (Oh, so good.) At Granddaddy's house, we slept on a feather bed. We would jump up and down until the mattress fell on the floor. We would put it back on the bed and go to sleep and it was good sleeping! Our younger cousin saw us playing with the mattress, and it looked like so much fun to her that she begged her mother to let her spend the night. Her mother said yes, and all of us had so much fun with the mattress. That changed about midnight when our cousin woke up crying for her mother. Lottie and I had to get up and walk her home about a half a mile in the pitch-black dark. Well, so much for company spending the night.

I have such great memories of the time we spent with my grand-daddy and our time on the farm. He was a fun granddaddy and very giving. I loved him. He really took care of his seven children. When my granddaddy had a birthday, instead of him getting something for his birthday, he would give every one of his children a thousand dollars. My mother sure did need it. I'm sure the other children did too. Oh, what great memories!

Chapter 9

Back to Our Home
Waldo Henderson's Still

Well, back at our house in Kirkland, one night, Lottie and I went to sleep, and about midnight, we heard a baby crying and I mean crying! I thought it would never stop. We couldn't figure out where the crying was coming from since we didn't have a baby. We were very surprised when we woke up the next morning. We had the most beautiful baby brother. I was eight years old and a proud big sister to Franklin James Holland. We now had someone to play with. We would swing him in the swing until he fell asleep, and then he would nearly fall out of the swing. When James was small, he had the whooping cough. Every night, he would cough so much, we were afraid he would lose his breath. We hated to see the night come because we were afraid something would happen to him. He finally overcame it, but it left him with asthma.

About three years later, we came home from school and as we climbed off the bus, a little boy said, "You will get a baby brother today."

Lottie shook her dinner bucket at him and said, "No!"

Daddy saw her shaking her bucket at him and tore Lottie up. That was really all it took for him to grab us up and whip us, especially if someone was looking.

Guess what? We did have another baby brother, and his name was Nerle; Nerle Eugene Holland. When James and Nerle got big enough for us to hold, it was our job to take care of them. I can't remember if I had James or Nerle. I probably had Nerle since he was the smallest. Lottie and James were plump. She probably felt more comfortable with him.

While Mama was busy taking care of babies, Daddy was busy as the wood rider. Daddy was not the only wood rider in our family. Daddy's sister, Aunt Vanna was married to Henry Lewis. Henry Lewis was also a wood rider working for a still.

One day, he went to the barber shop to get a haircut. The barber noticed a little pip on his right eye. Henry had not noticed it and it didn't bother him. Uncle Henry and the barber decided to just nip it off. Several weeks later, Uncle Henry noticed his eye was infected and was hurting him. He went to the doctor, and lo and behold, he had cancer. I remember he wore a black patch over his eye. The cancer really changed his life and his family's life. He tried to keep working, but it wasn't too long before the patch over his eye had to be made a lot larger to cover his nose and eye. This was a fast growing cancer. I can't remember too much because I was a little girl when this happened. This was the first case of cancer that I had heard of. I do know I heard my family talk about it all the time.

Uncle Henry and Aunt Vanna had three small daughters, and what would Uncle Henry do with no income? I remember my daddy packing up a big box of groceries from the commissary. Every Saturday, we would take the groceries to Willacoochee.

(see map number 4) where they lived. It was enough to last until the next Saturday. That was very meaningful to me for our family to help. Daddy's older brother and sisters chipped in too.

Uncle Henry and his family lived in a big two-story house right behind the stores in Willacoochee. Lottie and I, Wilford, and their three daughters, Pauline, Maude Lee, and Dorothy would play on the streets while Mama and Daddy would visit. Uncle Henry was getting worse. He was just lying in bed, knowing he was losing his eyes and nose. I'm sorry to say it wasn't long before Uncle Henry died. I had never heard of that kind of cancer before, but I'm sure there were more cases.

One time when we visited, Mama thought Pauline was big enough to have a pair of silk panties to cheer her up. The other girls were too small and didn't need any yet. Well, when I saw what she had done, I thought, *She gets silk panties and Lottie and I are still wearing flour-sack pants with that one piece of rubber and our one safety pin.* We were okay after Mama explained it.

Chapter 10

Moving to Douglas, Georgia

One day, Daddy came home and told us we were moving. All of us chimed in, "No!" We did not want to leave our big house where we played and had so much fun. My mama had beautiful flowers all over the big front porch, and she did not want to leave them. Mama could put a sprig of anything in dirt and make it grow. Daddy came home with a big old truck and put everything we had on it. Needless to say, Mama did lose nearly all her flowers.

When we arrived in Douglas (see map number 5), we saw this ugly, old, run-down shack with mud holes in the yard. There was no place to play, and it was in the poor section of town. We were upset and crying. Daddy talked to his boss man and told him what a mess it was. The next day or two, we were moved to a much nicer place. We were actually next door to the mayor's house. It had a porch all the way around it and was very nice.

The mayor's family was so nice. They had a girl who belonged to the mother and a boy who belonged to the father. They were two spoiled kids. The father was crippled and drove a small car called a Little Baby Austin. The mother was very nice to us. We were over at their house, playing, one day and they had a big bowl of apples on the table. They asked us if we wanted an apple. We were taught good manners and I said, "No."

I wanted one so badly. They were throwing them at each other like a ball. Those kids got apples all the time. We would never get apples except at Christmas. We would get one apple each year.

His wife did her good deed taking us to Sunday school. She would also give us a nickel to put in the collection plate. Now, nickels didn't come my way too often, and it took a lot of willpower to let it go. I wanted to put it in my pocket and keep it, but I didn't. I put it in the kitty (collection plate) at Sunday school and the teacher said to Johnny, "It is your time to have the money this morning." I thought if I had known he was going to get it, I would have kept my nickel. Well, maybe it will be my turn next. I later learned it was Johnny's turn to take the money to the collection plate, and he didn't get to keep the money.

It wasn't long before Daddy's boss man had a house built about three miles out of town and we moved into a new house. It was very nice. The turpentine still was a new still and close to our house. We played there all the time. It had a big round vat with nothing in it. One day, Wilford and Lottie talked me into getting down in it. I did get in it, and guess what? I couldn't get out of it. Wilford had to go get Mama and Daddy to come get me out. Needless to say, when my folks got a hold of me, that was the last time I got in that vat.

We had a patch of pine trees near our house. Daddy told my brother he could work that patch and have the money he made after school every day. He chipped the trees and put the cap up to collect the turpentine. He would go and clean it out and put it in the barrel and carry it to the still on his wagon. On Saturday, he got his pay of one dollar. He would take that dollar and ride on his bike about two miles to town and go to a movie. He would ride back home with a big ole smile on his face.

My other brothers, James and Nerle, had to catch a school bus to go to their school. It was cold while they waited on the school bus, so they would get a cup of resin and light it. This would keep them warm. When the bus came, they would put the fire out and hang the resin back on the tree until the next morning.

Chapter 11

McClellan School
Fifth Grade

We went to a three-room school named the McClellan School. I was in the fifth grade and made friends with a little girl about as poor as I was. She wanted me to go home with her after school. Mama let me go so we walked to her house. I didn't know she lived a mile from the school and it was cold, dead, winter time. I did not have a big, warm coat. We got to her house, and it was a shack with wind blowing through the cracks. All they had to eat was syrup and what I thought was biscuit but, no, it was cornbread. They had some kind of meat, but I really didn't know what it was. I soon found out. The kids were throwing stuff at each other at the table and something fell in my plate. In my syrup was a hog's eye. That saved me from eating the syrup and the cornbread that was on my plate.

Later that night, we had to go to bed to keep warm. We had six quilts on us. We couldn't even turn over, we were so bogged down, and it was still cold. I was so glad to get back to that schoolhouse and go back home after school to my warm house. I learned to appreciate my family and my home so much more after that little trip.

We had an old car in our backyard, and we played in it all the time. I remember one day, Mama had some words with a neighbor next-door by the name of Van Landing. Well, Mama ended up going and sitting in that old car and singing: "I may not be an angel, but angels are so few until the day that one comes along, I'll sing along with you."

Chapter 12

Aunt Rosa Lee

My mother had a sister named Rosa Lee. Rosa Lee moved to Texas and lived with relatives. She became a nurse. She would come home and visit with our family. When she came for her visit, we loved it. She always brought a big box of clothes with her. My sister and I couldn't wait to get into that box and see what we had.

Lottie looked in the box after I did, and she hollered, "Look, Evelyn, look what I found." I turned around to look and she was holding several pair of silk panties, our first ones!

I said, "Great, we can now throw away our old piece of rubber and safety pins." I had worn flour-sack panties until I was in the fifth grade, and I was ready for those silk panties.

Aunt Rosa Lee knew we were in need of clothes. What didn't fit us, my mother could make it fit. I didn't have a warm coat, and there was a coat in the box, but was too small for me. When Mother remade the coat, it *was* a coat of many colors. I was so proud to wear it.

Aunt Rosa Lee was so much fun to be around. She would always tickle me and my sister and pinch us on our breast and say, "They have grown some since I was here last year."

We would be embarrassed, but that was the way she was, and we loved her dearly. Aunt Rosa Lee got married and she and her husband had a baby girl named Jo Ann. She was their only child. Jo Ann now lives in my hometown of Fernandina with her husband, Winston Singletary. I see Jo Ann when I go to Fernandina.

Chapter 13

Camp Four, Dupont, Georgia
Sixth Grade

While at Dupont, family lived at Camp 4, now gone.
Found this old building still in the area.

Every time Daddy came home to say we're moving, it was exciting to us kids. We would get to explore another turpentine still. Most of the time, the stills looked the same. Some stills looked old and some looked new.

It was an adventure for us. The next year, someone offered Daddy five more dollars to go to another job, and off we went to Dupont, Georgia. (See map number 6.) This still was known all around as Camp Four. I was in the sixth grade at this time. I loved it at Camp Four. Every week, we would meet a rolling store at the commissary. We would each have a nickel, and I always got a moon pie. To this day, I love those pies. The rolling store was a truck that would come once a week with most anything we wanted. We never got to go to town so that rolling store was a treat for us.

We had a pretty nice house. In the house, the kitchen had a window above the sink. As Lottie and I did the dishes, we would prop a songbook in the window and sing. Mother didn't care how long it took us to do the job as long as we did it. Lottie always wanted to wash, and I would dry them and put them away. All the while we would sing and sing some more. Mother loved to hear us sing because we could harmonize pretty well.

One day at recess, we went and sat down by a tree and started singing just to have something to do. We never thought anyone was listening. A group of teachers heard us singing and loved it. Every Friday afternoon, the school had a program in the auditorium, and we were always on the program to sing.

I loved the sixth grade and we had a wonderful teacher. I wish I could remember her name. She is the teacher who taught me how to play the harmonica. The first song I ever played was "Home on the Range." I can see her now, waving her arm with a ruler in her hand. All the class would put our pointer finger over one key at a time and move over each key. That was a happy time in our class. We were invited to go to Homerville, Georgia, to play for a program. The morning of the program, I woke up with a toothache. Daddy took me to town and had my tooth pulled, and we made it to the program on time. I'll never know how I played with my tooth missing, but I did.

One day, Daddy came home with a mandolin and handed it to me to play. I said, "Why me? I've never seen one of those."

Daddy said, "You are the one I want to learn to play it."

Well, I banged on it and practiced until I learned two songs. I can't remember what the two songs were.

I took the mandolin to school and showed it to the teacher. She wanted me to play for her room. She also wanted me to play for the program we had every Friday afternoon. The day before I was to play,

I went home from school and my mandolin was gone. Daddy never did tell me what he did with it, but I bet he sold it. It was the end of my mandolin-playing career.

In DuPont, our house was very nice. We had a fire tower almost in our yard. All the kids would play on the first platform. Lottie and I would play with our dolls there. Daddy didn't like for us to go up there, but Mama didn't care. We could see very well from the fire tower. When we could see Daddy coming home, we would scoot down from up there.

Wooden fire tower that was at Camp 4 - where
Evelyn and sister Lottie played on steps.

The government had a work program that helped supply jobs for people. It was called the CCC. This boy who was in this CCC program, boarded with us and lived in the top of that fire tower. There was a play at the school and me and Lottie and Wilford wanted to go and Daddy didn't want to take us, so he asked the boy who was boarding with us to take us. He was a very nice guy.

Daddy asked him if he knew how to drive a car. The boy said, "Of course." Well, off we went, and about three miles from the house, he ran us into a ditch, and we couldn't get the car out. The three of us had to walk back to the house in pitch-black dark. The boy was so scared, he wouldn't leave the car. Daddy was asleep when we got back, and we didn't want to wake him. We waited to tell him about the car the next morning. He went to get the boy who had stayed by the car all night long. They got it out of the ditch and brought it home. Daddy was crazy about his car, and I hate to think what he said to that boy. Needless to say, the boy never drove us anywhere else again.

Chapter 14

Manor, Georgia on to Ousley, Georgia

There was a change in the wind, and you know what that meant. It was time for our family to move. We were moving to another turpentine still in Manor, Georgia (see map number 7).

The house we moved in was about ten feet from the highway and very small. The people who moved out of this house left their belongings packed in one room. We were not supposed to go near that room. We had the best time plundering in that room. We would never take anything, but we sure had a good time in there. That is about the only thing I remember in a way of a good time here. At this home in Manor, we had no lawn to play in or anywhere else to play. I hated that town. We go through this town nowadays on our way to Fernandina, but I could never find the house.

I was in the seventh grade, age twelve, and all the children here were bigger and taller than I was. They were a bunch of backwoods rednecks who did not want any new folks moving in to their town. No one was friendly here. We only stayed in Manor about three months, and we moved to Ousley, Georgia, just outside of Valdosta, Georgia. (See map number 3.)

We moved to Ousley in the summertime so we didn't go to a school, and I don't remember too much about this town. There is one thing that stands out. There was a railroad track that ran by the side of our house. There was a post office across the road from us. We would sit on our porch and watch the train go by and scoop up the mailbag with a hook and keep on going.

That was fascinating to me! I remember Uncle Elbert and Aunt Beulah came to spend the day with us and we were all playing. Aunt Beulah accidentally hit Daddy in the ribs and broke two of them. That is all I can remember about our time in Ousley, Georgia.

Chapter 15

Lenox, Georgia Eighth Grade

Our next move was to a little place name Mineola, Georgia, (see map number 9). In Mineola, we lived by a Presbyterian Church, and we actually went to church there some time. I went to school at Hahira, Georgia. I was in the seventh grade. Lottie and I had some friends who we went to Valdosta with. We just rode around and ate fruit. We didn't have a watch and we didn't know what time it was. When we got home it was late and Mama was waiting up for us. I was sick as a dog, so she didn't fuss so much. She ran the clock back an hour so Daddy wouldn't know what time it was. Thank goodness!

Evelyn at entrance to old Lenox School (now an Admin Office).

Our next move was up the way to Lenox, Georgia (see map number 10). I was about fourteen years old and in the eighth grade. We lived in a house called The Love Nest. It was so nice, but still no indoor bathroom. We sat on the throne of a nice, old outhouse and used the pages of Sears Roebuck book for our toilet paper.

I attended the outhouse frequently every time we had to work or do the dishes. Lottie would tell me, "You need not think you are getting out of washing the dishes because I am waiting on you." That she did.

Evelyn played basketball out in front of the Lenox school.

We walked to school in Lenox, and this is where I started playing basketball. I loved it. At this particular time in basketball, you had two forwards, two jump centers, and two guards. You played with two sections of the court. I was a forward and Lottie was a guard. We played in dresses outside on the dirt. After much practice, we became very good at basketball.

I met my first boyfriend in Lenox. His name was Joel Yawn. After a game one day, I went back in the schoolroom to get my books, and when I turned around, there was Joel. He had me backed into a corner and tried to kiss me. He did not succeed, but he sure scared me to death. He got so close it shook me up. I went home and was in a daze for days. Joel and I became close friends after that.

Chapter 16

Ty Ty, Georgia Taylor Still

Evelyn inside Ty Ty
current-day office.

Evelyn posing under
current-day plaque.

Ty Ty School is now Ty Ty City Hall.

The wind was changing and you know what that meant. We were moving again. We moved to Ty Ty, Georgia (see map number 11). Daddy worked for Mr. Everett Taylor at Taylor Still which was three miles from Ty Ty. We lived in a small white house next to Mr. and Mrs. Taylor and their children. We had no running water, nor did we have an indoor bathroom. During the day, we would sit two large tubs of water out in the sun so it would heat our water. We could have heated water if we sat the tubs on a wood stove that we cooked on. After dark, Lottie and I would take a bath in one tub of water.

It had been warmed up by the sun, and we would rinse off with the second tub of water. Then my brothers would do the same thing. I never lived in a house with a real bathroom until I graduated from high school. We had outhouses at every house. We also had a well or a pump at each house, and sometimes, in the winter, the pump would freeze. We would then have to heat water and pour over the pump to unfreeze it, and it took many trips to prime that pump.

Our house had a porch in front and our dining room had a window where you could look out to see the porch. My brother, Wilford, was a big ole comic and teaser. He also liked to get my goat. One afternoon, my boyfriend came to see me. Wilford held a cone of cornbread at the window for my friend to see. I was hoping the boy hadn't seen it, but he had. I told my friend that Wilford was having a little fun embarrassing me. That's the way we were. We always had a fun life. It seemed as if we were poor, but we didn't know it because we could always find something to make or something to do. We enjoyed playing together, joking with each other, and just having fun. This was one of those fun times.

Our house only had two bedrooms. My sister Lottie and I slept in one bed, and my brothers slept in another bed in the same room. There was a window at the head of the bed, and it was very hot in the summer. We did not have an air conditioner. You could buy these hand-held fans, and they were shaped like a man's head and neck. We would fan ourselves to sleep, and just before we would doze off, we would stand the fan up in the window.

One night Lottie had to go to the potty, and she had to crawl over me to get up. She looked up in the window and saw what she thought was a man's head, and she flopped right down on top of me, scared to death. I looked up and saw the same thing and I began to laugh.

I said, "Lottie, that's the fan."

We giggled all night and woke the boys up with all the commotion, and they started laughing with us. Mama came in the room to see what the laughing was all about in the middle of the night. We told her, and of course, she thought it was funny too. After a little while, she finally had us all get back to sleep.

One night, I needed to go to the outhouse, and Mama went with me because it was dark outside. While we were out there, I told Mama that one of the Taylor girls had told me that my mama was going to have a baby.

Well, Mama looked at me and said, "Yes, I am."

I was sixteen years old, and I didn't know she was pregnant. Mama had always had a big stomach, so I didn't notice she was pregnant. One night, not long after that, Daddy called the doctor, and he had to come from Tifton to see her. In the meantime, Mama woke us up and had Daddy take us down the road to Mrs. Taylor's house to stay until it was over. My mama had all her babies at home. This was the sixth child and the last.

We spent the night at Mrs. Taylor's. Daddy came after us the next morning and told us we had a brand-new baby brother. We were all so excited about this baby. Mama named him Vivian Burnell Holland. I helped Mother with him while he was growing up. All of us did.

Vivian Burnell Holland as a young boy

When I was sixteen and Lottie was fifteen, she had trouble with her tonsils. Mama took her to the doctor and he said, "We've got to get them out."

Mama didn't have the money to do it. The doctor knew of some organization that would pay for it. Mama thought if this is free, I better get Evelyn's tonsils out too. Lottie and I were so close that what one of us did, the other did too. All during grade school, Mama dressed us just alike. So, you know what happened? I got my tonsils out with Lottie.

At Mrs. Taylor's I would also baby-sit her children, and she would give me nice, new clothes for helping her. She knew if she gave me money, I would have no way of getting to town to buy anything. We did not have a car. Daddy could use the company truck, but he never took us to town. My daddy was a character. Sometimes he would leave on Friday night, and we would not see him home again until Sunday night. If he did happen to come back on Saturday night, he would have brought a piece of steak or liver, and Mama would cook it for his breakfast. Mama and kids would end up with the gravy from the steak or liver. We put the gravy on grits. We never had meat for us unless it was white-side meat from the commissary.

At Ty Ty, Lottie and I started playing basketball again. We were a good team, and we ended up playing against Excelsior School. I attended the tenth and eleventh grade years at Tifton High School until Christmas.

We needed a referee for this game, and we had to wait until a bus came from Tifton to bring a referee. When the bus pulled up, a nice-looking boy, about 250 pounds, stepped off the bus, and he refereed the game.

Vernon Shaw

The referee's name was Vernon Shaw. Vernon's sister, Frances, played for the opposite team. Her team beat us, and we blamed it on the referee!

We continued playing basketball in Tifton. Tifton turned the gym into a voting precinct, but up in the attic, you can see the original gym rafters where we played basketball in the picture.

Evelyn played basketball in the Tifton High School gym (now a voting precinct).

Evelyn even remembered the location of Coach Thompson's office.

The gym ceiling was lowered; however, the old wooden rafters can still be seen in the top of the existing building.

Chapter 17

Vernon Shaw Enters My Life

I played basketball for Tifton. We had a school club called The T Club. In order to be in the club, you had to be initiated. The club girls initiated me, all right! They made me wear a short dress with painted freckles on my face. They put lard in my hair, and I had to carry a dinner plate around all day with the letter T in the plate. I also had to go up on stage and play the tune, "That Little Boy of Mine" on my harmonica and dedicate it to "Puny Shaw." I really didn't know who he was, but I knew he was a big 250-pound football player in Tifton.

Somehow we ended up in the same English class and he sat right behind me. He stole a picture of me out of my book. This guy who sat across from him in class dared him to ask me for a date. He told Vernon he would give him $5 if he asked me out. Well, he asked me, and I accepted. Some people would do anything for that kind of money. He knew that would help fill his car with gas. We ended up going to movies on our date, and we topped it off with hamburgers. We had a great time.

Tifton High School is now a City Administration Building.

Vernon asked me to go to the high school banquet. We did not have proms back then; he waited till almost time for the banquet to ask me. I did not have a dress or shoes or hose or make-up or finger-nail polish or anything else as far as that matters. Did I dare say yes? I told him I would let him know. I went to Mary Lou Taylor's and asked her if she had a dress I could wear. She told me she didn't. She wanted me to be able to go to that banquet, so she went to Tifton and bought material for a dress. The material was pink-dotted Swiss and beautiful. She bought a pattern for an evening gown. She gave it to Mama, and Mama went to sewing on my evening gown day and night. This gown also had a little short jacket that went with the dress.

The day Vernon was to pick me up, Mary Lou Taylor came over and gave me the works. She polished my nails and put makeup on me. I wore Mama's white sandals and hose. When Vernon came to the door and saw me, I thought he would faint. Vah-vah-va-boom! He had never seen me so pretty. When we arrived at the banquet, his football buddies were as surprised as he was. I think they envied him. We had a good time. We sat at the head table because he was a big football player. We really thought we were the cat's pajamas!

When I started dating Vernon in the ninth grade, we went to different places. Every Friday night, someone in our class at school would have something at their house. We took turns: one would have a peanut boiling, a corn shucking, and cane peeling. We made it fun just sitting around a fire and cracking and eating peanuts. We would talk and tell stories and laugh. The parents would serve lemonade or Kool-Aid and some crackers. The class members were mostly from farms, and we would have good ole sugar cane peelings and sit around and chew on the cane while we talked. When it came my turn to have everybody over, we had a marshmallow roast. My brother, Wilford, had built a big swing in our front yard. We took turns swinging and some couples would take a walk down the road and back.

One night, Vernon was invited to a dance in a little town outside of Tifton in Chula. It was a square dance. Everybody got in a big circle and danced around the room. We would change partners ever so often. There would be a caller who yelled out during dance moves. When the guy called do-si-do, I just loved it! I was having a great time, and all of a sudden, my foot and entire leg fell through a hole in the floor up to my yin-yang! I was so embarrassed. Vernon was way across the room with another girl, and I was so glad he didn't see me do that. I got out of the hole with the help of my partner, and I didn't get hurt. I was just shocked and embarrassed. We courted several months having a great time. I really did like him. He was cute, nice, and he treated me with respect. One night, we could not agree on something, and we had a fuss. He broke up with me, and I was brokenhearted.

As time moved on, I dated other boys. Lottie and I had a date one Sunday night, and we were going to church. When the boys arrived, my daddy was sitting on the porch, trimming his toenails. As we were leaving, Daddy asked, "Where do you two think you are going?"

We told him to church.

He said, "No, you are not. If these boys can't come see you in the daytime, they are not taking you out at night."

Well, Ms. Lottie said, "Yes, we are going. Come on, Evelyn."

So I tagged along, and we went to church and came home. When we got back, Daddy was waiting for us with the biggest stick I've ever seen. He drew back to hit Lottie and my brother jumped out of bed and grabbed the stick away from him. Of course, that made Daddy very mad, and they started fighting. Well that didn't end so well. Daddy told Wilford to leave and not come back. When Wilford jumped out of bed to grab the stick, he only had on pajamas. Now, he was having to leave the house in only his pajamas. Daddy put Wilford out in the cold with no clothes. Wilford decided he would go next door to Daddy's boss man and tell him what happened. They let Wilford stay there that night. The next day, Mr. Taylor fired my daddy. We hated it because we were going to have to move.

Chapter 18

Queensland, Georgia

We did move and this time to a town called Queensland, Georgia. It was about five miles outside of Fitzgerald, Georgia (see map number 12). Daddy found another job. We lived in a very small house that had another small house in front of it. Wilford slept there.

When we moved to Queensland, we were not doing so well. The commissary food was getting old. We needed something different to eat. Daddy hired James to take care of the water tank, and James hired Nerle to help him.

James Holland

Nerle Holland

The boys were really at a loss here for something to do. This gave them a chance to stir around, and no one noticed what they were doing. We had chickens roaming around the yard all over the place.

James and Nerle would just lead one of those chickens right to our house. They were leading a chicken a day, and we were having chicken for supper. It sure was good! As the chickens sort of dwindled down, they started locking those chickens up. We had to go back to eating commissary food. We never bought groceries in a grocery store until I graduated from high school. We had never even seen one!

When Vernon found out we were moving, he made a beeline to see me, and we got back together. I was so happy about that. I really liked him. We had a hard time trying to get together. He never knew when he could get his family's car and could never really make a date. One night, he came to Fitzgerald to see me, and I was already asleep. Mama woke me up and helped me dress. She had me brush my teeth and sent me out the door to be with him. She liked him and trusted him with me. I liked him too!

The school in Fitzgerald would not let us go to school there because we had moved so much. My grades and units could not catch up with me. They did not believe I was in the eleventh grade. It was Christmas time when we moved there, and I only had five months left before I would graduate. In those days, our school only went to the eleventh grade. Mother thought it best if I went and stayed with my uncle, her brother, in order to finish school on time.

Chapter 19

Mystic High School My Senior Trip

Mystic School is now the
Mystic City Hall.

Evelyn posing under Mystic School
plaque.

In Mystic, Georgia (see map number 1), I enrolled at Mystic High
School while living with my uncle. I could graduate in five months.
I did do that, and several weeks before I graduated, the class talked
about a trip to Washington, DC. That was an exciting thought to
me, but I had the choice between a trip and a class ring. I chose to
go on the trip. All the class had to work hard to be able to afford this
trip. We sold candy for a fundraiser, and we made enough to pay for
our trip. When the time finally came for our trip, everyone gathered
at the school and said our goodbyes to our parents and then boarded
our school bus. We settled in on the bus and headed for Atlanta,
Georgia, on May 29, 1941.

Our first stop was in front of the Fox Theater. As we were getting off the bus, everyone saw smoke coming from under the bus.
While we were seeing the show at the Fox, the bus driver was finding
someone to check out the bus. When we got out of the theater, we
did not see our bus. We did see a large hotel across the street with

some rocking chairs on the front porch. While waiting for the bus, all of us, including the teacher, started rocking on the porch. We rocked for about an hour before the bus driver came and took us to our hotel for the night.

We started out early the next day en route to Washington, DC. We had reservations at a boarding house called Elizabeth Willard's. We arrived there late in the afternoon and got ready for a tour bus early the next morning. We went to the Capitol. Congress was in session, but we missed our representative, Representative John S. Gibson of the 77th Congress. He later sent me a letter and a picture of him. It was dated August 13, 1941. I still have his letter and picture in my scrap book.

We saw so many sights in Washington. Among them were the Washington Monument, Lincoln Memorial, Smithsonian Institute, and the White House. We also saw the changing of the guards at Arlington National Cemetery. We even went to Mt. Vernon to see where George Washington lived.

Our tour bus was fast. We covered everything in a day. The next morning, we were going to leave to start home, and guess what? The bus would not start. Luckily, the bus driver could take care of this problem.

Well, we were heading home. My daddy had only given me ten dollars to go on the trip, and when it came time to stop at a nice restaurant, we had to pay for it. I let someone talk me into getting deviled crab. I didn't like it, so I went home hungry. I had spent my last dollar. All in all, it was a great trip, and I enjoyed it.

Chapter 20

My Solo Move

After graduating from Mystic High School, I went back home. I found out about a government program for underprivileged children called National Youth Association (NYA). I qualified for that, so I was soon to be moving again. I packed my tacky little dress and my tacky little hat and my ragged old suitcase. I sat by the highway and flagged down a bus. I was off on a new adventure to Milledgeville, Georgia (see map number 13). I enrolled at Georgia State College for women (GSCW), a well-known school for girls.

When I arrived at the big city, I signed in at GSCW. I was taken to a large, two-story beautiful house. The house would house eighteen girls, and a couple who were to be our house parents. We called them Mom and Pop Peters. At the school, our schedule was unusual. One week we went to class, and the next week we were taught skills such as meal planning, cooking, cleaning, and sewing. I made a dress for myself during these classes. We also had regular classes, such as English, math, history, and so forth. I remember one of the girls that attended the school. Her name was Mary Cline. She was from Leesburg, Georgia. For some reason, Mary really liked me, and everywhere I went, there was Mary. Her parents sent her packages with candy, and Mary would not share her candy with anyone else but me.

While at the school, we had to choose an occupation, but we didn't have many choices. I chose to learn to make salads at the college kitchen. I looked up one day, and there stood Mary. For some reason, that girl irritated me, so I decided I would change from salad making to ceramics. I had to walk over to the boys' college to take that class. It seemed to me that would be more interesting than cutting up lettuce. I loved the ceramic class, and I was working away one day. Guess what? I looked up, and there stood Mary! I decided at that point to learn to accept Mary. If she loved me that much, I guess I could learn to love her too, and I did.

We had some boys in the ceramic class that we really enjoyed, so you can believe that was better than cutting up that old lettuce. We truly had a great time playing in the mud and clay and making ash trays, little jugs, lamps, and plates.

My ceramic jug that I made in my class

Unfortunately, no sooner that we settled in at the school and began to make progress, the government representative contacted our house parent and told them the program would be cancelled. All the girls came together like a bunch of sad-sacks and cried and cried. We started packing our old suitcases, and Mom and Pop Peters took us to the bus station. At the bus station, we had another big crying spell and it all came to an end. We hugged everyone goodbye. No sooner than my school career started, it ended.

When I was dating Vernon, his parents lived on a big farm in the Excelsior Community.

Old Home Place where Vernon was born

This community had a country store, a school, and a bunch of farmers. Vernon was born there in their farmhouse. His family farmed there until the boys grew up. There was just too much work on the farm to continue it. They sold the farm and moved to Tifton, Georgia. This was a big city for the country farmers. Papa James and Grandma Bessie liked living in the city, but they missed their friends in the country.

Chapter 21

Visiting Tifton

While I was in school, my family moved to Fernandina Beach, Florida (see map number 14). After I left school, I decided I would go to Fernandina and be with my family. Since Vernon and I had still been writing to each other, I thought on the way to Fernandina, I would take a bus trip to Tifton and visit with him and his family. It turned out to be great. I loved my time with him and his family. I can remember one great day with them. Frances, Vernon's Sister, knew how much her mama missed her friends from the country, so she planned all of us an outing. A long time ago, people would come in to town from the country and visit on the downtown streets. Tifton downtown is where the country folks would gather on Saturdays. The streets would be so full, you could hardly walk. If you didn't get a parking place early in the morning, you would have a long way to walk to get to Main Street. Frances decided to surprise Mama Bessie and take her to town. Frances took the car to town and parked it in front of the theater which was the main part of town. She took a taxi back to the house. After lunch, we called a cab to come and get us and take us to our car. Now Mama Bessie had a front-row seat to see all her friends come strolling by. In those days, they didn't have parking meters.

the Tift Theatre as a photo on display in the theater's
over the years. The marquee in the older picture ha
ovie.

travis.hatfield@albanyherald.com

Downtown Tifton, Georgia

Frances and Evelyn on a sunshiny day

One hot afternoon, Frances and Vernon's sister-in-law Pauline and I decided we would go swimming in a creek. This creek is where all the people at their country church would go to be baptized. It was a great little swimming hole. We were having so much fun that we never noticed the time. We did not mean to stay so long, and I got red all over my back, face, and shoulders. Suntan lotion was not heard of in those days. We doctored it the best we could when we got home. Unfortunately, I was leaving the next morning on a bus from Tifton, Georgia, to Fernandina Beach, Florida, and I could not lean back in the seat. You know I was really looking forward to getting home and letting my mother dress it.

While I was in school at GSCW, Vernon was working at a filling station in Tifton after high school. When I had stopped to visit him, he told me he had just joined the navy. I was sad about that. He would be leaving for Norfolk, Virginia, while I was leaving for Fernandina. Vernon told me it would be several months before he saw me again, and if I wanted to date while he was gone, he wouldn't be mad. He did say for me to remember him and know that he loved me and always would.

Chapter 22

Fernandina Beach, Florida

The Coast Guard was a great place to meet guys. I did date some of the Coast Guard guys who were stationed in Fernandina. I would go to the movies on a date, and I would take my baby brother, Burnell, with me. He was five years old. The guys did not seem to mind. I would tell them straight-up that I was engaged and I was. Vernon had sent me an engagement ring through the mail. It was a great surprise. In the navy, Vernon moved around a lot and when he left Norfolk, he came to Jacksonville, Florida. Jacksonville is only thirty miles from Fernandina, so we got to see each other twice while he was there. After Jacksonville, they sent Vernon back to Norfolk, but he didn't stay there very long.

When I arrived in Fernandina, Daddy had me a job in a drug store. It was not my idea of a job, but I did go to work there, and I stayed there three years. I would go in early in the morning before the light of day. We lived just two blocks from the drug store. The store was on the corner and easy to find. I had to walk to work in the dark, and I mean dark; but the cook was always waiting for me to open the door. I worked until one o'clock and would be off until five o'clock. We had a luncheonette in the drug store, and we served breakfast and lunch. My first week at work, I had a problem. I would sell a ten-cent cup of coffee and the customer would give me a dollar to pay for it. I would give them back nine dimes or eighteen nickels for change. My boss finally caught on that I was giving all his change away. He pulled me aside and said, "Let me teach you how to make change for a dollar." You know, I had never had a dollar in my life to know how to make change.

While I was off the few hours in between shifts, I made good use of my time. If I had the money, I would go the cloth store and buy a yard of material to make a "broomstick" skirt.

Broomstick Skirt

When I went back to work, I had a new skirt. I was pretty good on a sewing machine, and all I had to do was gather the skirt at the top, put a band on it, and hem it. I made quite a few skirts. The cloth cost twenty-five cents a yard.

When I worked at the drugstore in Fernandina, I had a friend named Lila who also worked at the drugstore. One day, she had the day off, so I decided to call her just to talk. There was no particular reason. She came to the phone which was in the hall of her house and she didn't say hello. She hollered, "Evelyn, my house is on fire!" I told her to hang up and get out of the house, and I would call the fire department. The fire department got to her house in time to save it. I feel like something told me to call her that day.

While we were working at the drugstore, Lila was courting Mac McJunkin. Mac owned the bus station and had plenty of money. Lila and I would get together and decide on something we wanted. One day, we decided we wanted a horse. Mac got the horse for us. His bus station was at the end of Main Street and it had an empty lot on it. That's where he kept the horse. One day, I decided I was going for a ride. Mac saddled the horse and put me on it. (I'd never ridden a horse in my life!) I was going to go across Main Street and go to a back street where there were no cars. My horse had another idea. The horse started down Main Street, galloping as fast as he could. When he went up, I went down. I was hollering, "Help, please stop this horse!" A man ran out and got a hold of him and helped me get off. I've never gotten on a horse again.

After working at the drugstore for three years, I was offered a job in the office of Rainier Pulp Mill and I took it. After I had been at the job a few months, all the girls working there found out I was engaged, so they gave me a shower. They went together and bought me one gift. It was a twenty-one piece set of crystal.

My china that was given to me in 1943.

Now, for a country girl to know what to do with them, I had no idea. I packed them up in 1945 and put them in my cedar chest that Vernon had given me.

When Vernon left Norfolk, he went to many places before he ended up at Bremington, Washington Naval Base. He was being prepared to go to the South Pacific. In 1942, he boarded the United States Navy Ship, The USS *Enterprise*. I did not see him again for three solid years.

I continued working at the paper mill while Vernon was away at the war. In Fernandina, during this time, my daddy was working a new job. The turpentine business was slowly going away. Daddy got a job during the war walking a pipeline around the city. When the war ended, he went to work at the Sheriff's Office. Guess what his job was? Hunting down bootleggers! We had fun with that one. He stayed with the Sheriff's Office about six months, and after his bout with bootleggers came to a close, he went to work in Jacksonville, Florida, working at the shipyard. He worked five days a week and drove back and forth, until one day, a barge ran into the drawbridge going into Fernandina. The road that was hit was the only way in and out of Fernandina, so we were actually stranded on the Fernandina side for about six months.

Daddy had to get a room and stay in Jacksonville until they could get a rowboat to take people on the island. They stopped the boat at midnight. If you missed the boat, you would have to spend the night in Jacksonville. After the bridge was fixed, Daddy still stayed over in his room, and that is where he had his first stroke. He fell on the floor and stayed there until one of his friends found him and called an ambulance. The ambulance took Daddy to the Fernandina Hospital. He was paralyzed all the way down his left side, legs, arms, and the left side of his face. At that time, he smoked cigarettes. I can remember the cigarette would burn the left side of his mouth because he could not feel anything.

I don't remember how long he stayed in the hospital, but when he finally came home, he was in a wheelchair. Not only did Mother have to take time off from work, all of us had to help out. Mama was working as a helper at the cafeteria at the high school at that time. She now had to work, work, and work at home. She took care of Daddy and even shaved him with a straight-blade razor.

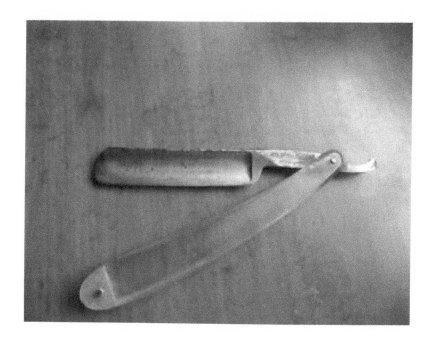

Straight-blade razor

She worked with him every day to get him up and out of that wheelchair. I was also helping out by working. My brothers James and Nerle were helping out as much as they could. Our family pulled together to help my daddy walk again, and he did!

Chapter 23

My Wedding

In 1945, Vernon's ship was hit by a Japanese plane and had to be taken back to the naval base in Washington State for repairs. While it was being repaired, they let the boys come home on a thirty-day leave. Vernon caught a bus and rode for a solid week all the way across the USA to get to Fernandina. I met him at the Jacksonville bus station. Vernon told me he would be coming in on a Greyhound bus at a certain time. I was looking out for him, and of course, the bus was running late. A group of ladies were there waiting for their loved ones too. When the bus arrived, the door opened, and a group of navy guys started coming off that bus. I couldn't see Vernon. I thought everyone was off the bus, and I still didn't see Vernon, and I was about to cry. I looked up one more time, and there was this one last soldier coming off the bus. He was taking his time. He stood at the door looking at me. I was looking up at this soldier, and I was looking for a two-hundred-and-fifty pound sailor. This soldier was a dark, redheaded man and very slim. He was smiling at me as he came closer. I was just about to cry because I thought my man had missed the bus. All of a sudden, I realized it was Vernon! He had sure put a scare in me. This new man was one hundred eighty five pounds! I grabbed him and put my arms round his waist. That was the first time I had ever been able to do that!

"What has the navy done to you?" I asked.

He said, "Not done *to* me, but *for* me. When I went into the navy, I weighed two hundred fifty pounds. They did not have a uniform to fit me. I had to wear my own clothes until they could make me a couple of uniforms."

I could not believe how different he looked and for the good. He was so handsome! Vernon told me he wanted to surprise me. He sure did!

We had little time to spare before we caught another bus to Fernandina. There was a park across from the bus station, and we went over there and found a shady spot on a park bench. This is the spot where Vernon got on his knees and asked me to marry him. Well, after waiting three years and receiving 197 letters from him, I said, "Yes!"

Love Letters 1941-1943

Vernon had come in on Friday, and we had to wait three days before we could get married. We married on Monday, July 16, 1945.

We did not have any time to get the church ready, but all my friends got together and went to work. We got married in the First Baptist Church of Fernandina Beach, Florida. The church was having a revival that week, so we had plenty of people at our wedding. We had not had time to invite anyone to the wedding, including his family. My brother James was Vernon's best man, and my best friend, Marie Thornton, was my maid of honor.

We left the church in a Greyhound Bus and went to St. Augustine, Florida, for a week on our honeymoon. We stayed in the Alhambra Hotel, and every time we came out the door, there was a man driving a buggy for visitors. That man did not go to anyone else the whole week but us. We saw everything there was to see in St. Augustine. It was a great week.

We left there and went to Tifton to see his folks and told them we were married. They were so happy for us. I wish there had been time to invite everyone to the wedding. I would have loved for them to have been there.

Vernon was supposed to have thirty days leave, but they called him back in two weeks to the naval base in Washington State. It took him a week on the bus to get back. No sooner than he got to Washington State, they sent him to the Chicago Naval Base, so he had to get back on a bus and ride another whole week from Washington State to Chicago. When he settled in at the base in Chicago, they made Vernon take swimming lessons every night. Now, that did not make a bit of sense. He had been on the ocean on a ship for three years, and now they want him to have swimming lessons?

Chapter 24

Moving Away from My Home and the South

I was still in Fernandina working and helping Mama rehab Daddy. He was not strong after the first stroke and would still have his struggles. In the meantime, Vernon was in Chicago. He wanted me to come and be with him. He looked for an apartment for us and finally found one. I made the decision to go and be with Vernon. I left my daddy sick in his bed, begging me not to go. That was a hard decision for me to make.

My mom said, "Go and take care of your husband, and I will take care of mine."

I decided to go, and I said goodbye to my dad and told him I'd see him soon. Mama and Daddy continued rehabbing Daddy until he could get along much better.

Chapter 25

My Dad

On November 11, 1945, Veterans Day fell on a Sunday, so the town would celebrate Veterans Day on Monday. They had a man running for governor who was coming to town for the Veterans Day program to make a speech. Daddy walked downtown to hear him speak. We only lived two blocks from town. Daddy walked back home and sat down on the couch to tell Mama about some of the funny things the man said.

All of a sudden, he looked at Mama and said, "My eyes are feeling funny. I can't see."

Mama said, "Do you want to go and lie down?"

Daddy said, "I believe I do."

They left the living room and had to walk through the dining room and the kitchen before getting him in the bedroom. By the time she got him in the bedroom and lying down, Daddy shut his eyes and passed away.

My daddy passing away left my mother with three boys to take care of all by herself. James was fifteen, Nerle was eleven, and Burnell was five. Daddy did not have life insurance to help with the funeral. He did have ten brothers and sisters, and they took up a collection at his funeral to pay the funeral home. They also gave Mama some money to help with the household expenses and the boys. Someone told Mama about getting Social Security, so she applied for it, and received a check; that was a big help. Mama also got a job cleaning the First Baptist Church.

James was fifteen and was going into high school. He played football after school, but on Saturday, he worked all day at a Jot-Em-Down Store. The job really came in handy because during the time Daddy was sick. They had created a big grocery bill. There was a grocery store in front of our house, and it was easy to run over there and get what was needed and charge it. The bill had gotten pretty big, so James told Mama not to worry about that bill. He would take care of it. He did take care of Mama and the bill. He continued working odd jobs until he got out of high school and then he got a job at the paper mill. He really could make money now to help out.

My oldest brother, Wilford, was in the army in Germany at the time of Daddy's death. The Red Cross was supposed to have gotten word to Wilford about Daddy, but they had not. So when the war ended, Wilford was coming home and did not know that Daddy had died. He was coming home with presents, and he had a present to give to Daddy, a watch.

Wilford had brought me a present as well. They saved it for me. It was a pitcher, sugar dish, and creamer. It was china inside and was covered with something like silver on the outside.

This gift meant the world to me. I still have it today in my cedar chest. I have never seen one like it. He brought it all the way from Germany. As soon as Wilford got back and settled down, he went right to work at the paper mill so he could help out as well.

As far as my having left Fernandina to go to Chicago to be with Vernon, I had no idea when I told Daddy I was leaving that he would pass away four months later. Daddy died of a stroke at age forty-seven. When I left for Chicago, that was the last time I ever saw my daddy.

Chapter 26

My Chicago Days with Vernon

When I left Fernandina, I caught a bus to Jacksonville and caught another bus to Chicago, Illinois. I have a hard time believing I did this all by myself. I was so timid, and I didn't think I could do this, but I did. Vernon couldn't meet me at the bus station, so I took a taxi and went to the apartment. The ride cost me twenty dollars.

When Vernon came home that night, he asked me how I liked the apartment he had gotten for us. I told him, "Yes, anything would have been okay just so I could be with you."

The so-called apartment was one room with a bed and straight chair and a Chester drawer to put my clothes in. There was no place in the one room to hang any clothes. We had kitchen privileges, so now I had to cook. Wow! I didn't know what he liked. I didn't know where to start. I was a young bride not used to cooking. Now, I was in someone else's kitchen. I grew up making coffee in a percolator. This kitchen had a drip coffeepot which I didn't know a thing about. I'd pour water in it and expect it to perk up over the coffee. It would run over the pot and spill all over the stove and floor. I'd clean it up and try again. One day, the lady we rented from must have seen that I didn't know what I was doing, and she said, "Honey, let me show you how to make coffee." She made my day!

Vernon and I were hungry for some good ole southern fried chicken. I went to the grocery store and called myself getting a fryer to cook. I got the smallest one they had. Those northern folk don't know what a fryer is. I bought the chicken anyway and cooked it so pretty and brown and had it on the table when Vernon came in. We sat down to eat. I took a bite of my chicken, and it was raw on the inside. I put it down and looked at Vernon. He was chewing on his piece. I do believe he would have eaten the whole thing raw before he would hurt my feelings. I told him, "Honey, you do not have to eat that." He put it down in a hurry.

We didn't get any chicken that night. I fried it again the next night, and it was good. Some nights, Vernon had to stay at the Naval Post. I would go on a trolley to meet him. We would go to a movie together. I would have to come back home by myself, and I had to walk two blocks after I got off the trolley. I was scared one night. I thought I heard footsteps behind me, and I ran as fast as I could and couldn't get the key in the door fast enough.

We rented from a middle-aged couple, and he worked at night and slept in the daytime. She worked all day. I was a young lady staying at home all day with nothing to do. She had a big bookcase full of books, so I read all day. There was no television at this time and no radio either. The lady would call me all day long to see what I was doing. I guess she thought I was spending time with her husband.

One night, Vernon came home very sick. He had the worst cold from taking swimming lessons every night. Before he came home, his boss man told him to go by a liquor store and get a pint of whiskey. He told him to drink all of it and get in the bed and sleep it off. That's exactly what he did, but he was not used to drinking. In the middle of the night, he had nightmares, and I couldn't keep him in the bed. I had to get on top of him and straddle him. We stayed that way for the rest of the night. He was completely out of it, but sure enough, the next morning, he was okay. He had sweated it out during the night and no more cold.

One night, we went to the movie, and when they turned on the lights, we were the only white couple in the theater. We were not used to that.

Another night, we decided to go out on the town. I dressed up, and we caught a trolley. It was sort of like a trolley, and we could ride it anywhere for just ten cents a piece. That sure beat taking a taxi for twenty dollars. We went to a fancy club and it had a big ballroom. We ate dinner and danced, but never noticed the time. We got ready to catch the trolley to go home, and it had stopped running for the night. We had to walk ten blocks home! We really didn't care because we were young and in love. We just moseyed along and looked at the moon and just had fun. We were pretty tired when we got home, and my feet sure did hurt.

Chapter 27

I Returned to Tifton to Help

I had been in Chicago about three months when we got a call from Vernon's mother. She called to say Frances, Vernon's sister, was very sick. She was in the Veterans Hospital in Moultrie, Georgia. Papa James and Grandma Bessie had to keep her little boy and drive back and forth to Moultrie to see about her. They needed help. Vernon packed me up and sent me to Tifton to stay with his parents and Frances's son. While I was in Tifton, a wonderful thing happened. The war was declared over! Glory hallelujah! Vernon would be coming home soon!

One night Ronnie, Frances and Bill's son, was eating supper, and there was a knock on the front door. I went to see who it was, and I opened the door and there stood Vernon. I screamed with delight, of course. It scared Ronnie, and he wouldn't let Vernon get close to me.

Frances finally got better. They dismissed her from the hospital, and not long after that, Ronnie and Frances left and went back home to be with her husband Bill. A few years later, Frances and Bill had a beautiful little girl. They named her Karen. At the present time, Karen lives in Watkinsville, Georgia, and has a beautiful family. I have visited with Karen and her family, as well as Ronnie and his wife, Judi, especially when Frances was living.

Vernon and I stayed with Mama Bessie and Papa James about a month. Vernon was looking for a job. One day, a friend asked Vernon if he would like a job working with Nabisco driving a truck. Vernon said he would take it while he looked for something else. Nabisco had a warehouse in Tifton (see map number 15) to save gas during the war.

Chapter 28

Life in Tifton, Georgia

Mama Bessie and Papa James (Vernon's Parents)

Mama Bessie and Papa James home on
South Park Avenue in Tifton, Georgia

Vernon's parents were great to us. They were in no hurry for us to leave, but I wanted Vernon and me to have our own place. One day, while Vernon was working, I got a cab and went to town. I found a newspaper with ads, and I found an apartment for rent. When Vernon got home, we went and looked at the apartment. It was really a big house with a hall down the middle. One side of the house was for rent. It included a big bedroom and living room all-in-one with a potbelly stove for keeping warm. It had a big kitchen and bathroom. On the back porch was a wringer-washer for washing clothes.

Vernon hadn't had time to look for another job, so he stayed with Nabisco, making good money. He made a big ole whopping eighteen dollars a week, five days a week. Vernon got paid on Mondays, and we were always broke by the weekend. We would go out on the porch and swing and watch the cars go by. (Fun, fun!)

One month, I had saved a one-dollar bill, and in my mind, I should have spent it on so many things that we needed.

This one Saturday, we were sitting on the porch, swinging, and I looked at Vernon and said, "What would you say if I told you I had a dollar bill?"

He said, "Go get it and let's go to the movies."

Guess what? That is what we did, and we saw two movies and had two drinks and a big bag of popcorn out of that one dollar bill! We had five cents left over. Oh, for the good ole days!

We lived in that apartment for about six months. I got a job at a drugstore in Tifton on Main Street. I worked until I found out I was pregnant. I had a friend who was pregnant at the same time. I would call her each day to check on her. I was asking if she was ready to have her baby because she was due before me.

One day, my water broke and I was sitting on the chamber pot when it happened.

I called her and said, "Guess what? I am ready to have this baby."

She said, "No, you are not!"

I convinced her I was, but she said, "No, you are not supposed to go before me." I told her I was on my way.

I stayed on the chamber pot until Vernon got there and took me to the Tifton Hospital. They put me to bed and prepared to shave me and get me ready for the baby to come. In the meantime, they looked at me and saw a little foot sticking out, so they got busy and called the doctor. I was in the hospital during the World Series and the doctor was looking at the ballgame when the nurse had to call him to come to the hospital. He came to the hospital and Dwain was born in twenty minutes.

The doctor came out and talked to Vernon.

He said, "What's the score?"

Vernon said, "Score? Hell, how's my wife and baby?"

The doctor said, "They are fine and you have a little boy."

Dwain was born breach, his feet first, and they couldn't get his head out. In so doing, the doctor put his finger in his mouth, pulled on his head, and injured the muscles in his neck. It took several months before we noticed his head was cocked. One ear sat one inch ahead of the other. The right side of his head was flat, and Dwain could turn his head to the left, but could not turn to the right. We took him to his doctor when we discovered it.

The doctor said, "Oh. Don't get worried. He will grow out of it."

Dwain did not grow out of it. He walked with his head turned to one side.

Chapter 29

Our Move to Thomasville

Vernon came in from work one day and said, "Well, we are going to have to move."

I said, "Where and why?"

Vernon told me they were moving the Nabisco warehouse to Thomasville, Georgia (see map number 16). They were closing the one in Tifton.

Well, where do I start? We made a quick trip to Thomasville to hunt an apartment. The only one we could find had a bedroom and kitchen. The bedroom was so very small. We had a hallway and a baby bed. We put the dresser drawer under the stairway. We had a baby who used cotton diapers (no Pampers in those days). I had to wash diapers and our clothes, but the landlord said we could not wash our clothes. She did not tell us that before we moved in. I would slip around and wash our clothes, but the landlord would catch me. She told me I would have to buy a fuse every time I washed clothes.

I really got tired of that mess. I was so sick of that apartment. I went to town one day and met a friend for lunch. I was telling her about the apartment, and she asked me if I had heard about the houses on North Hansel Street. The VA was making small houses for servicemen. I told her I had not, but I would check into it. When Vernon came home from work, we drove over and looked at the homes. They were not the fanciest houses, but to us it was heaven. I had never had a nice house because we had moved so many times. This house was so pretty to me. It had a living room, a dining room, and a kitchen. On the other side, it had two bedrooms and a bath in between. It would be just right for us. The next few weeks, we went to work on paperwork and bought us a house for $3,000.

Chapter 30

Our First Home:
Hansel Street
Thomasville, Georgia

Our very first home in Thomasville, Georgia

We gladly left that apartment and moved to our new house on North Hansel Street. We had no furniture for the living room, and Vernon's boss man gave us a nice dining room set with six chairs. We had a bed and a baby bed. We loved the house. Every room was a different color. They used Kem Tone paint, which was cheap. We had a pink, blue, and yellow room. We would stand back and look at it. It was so pretty.

The backyard was nothing but weeds, grass and trees up to the back door. We had to work in the yard every chance we had to get the yard cleared. One day, while we were pulling up weeds and picking up the trash, I went inside the house to get a drink of water. While I was washing my hands and looking at my rings on my finger, I took another look real quick. There was no ring! While clearing the yard, I must have lost my diamond out of my engagement ring. I was sick, and I went back outside and told Vernon. He was sick too. We never looked for it. In all the mess we had outside, we knew we would never find it. After buying the house, we just couldn't afford to replace it. I put my ring away until we could replace it. Several years later, we did get a zircon to replace the one I lost. I am proud to say many years later, on my twenty-fifth wedding anniversary, Vernon gave me a new set of rings!

We loved our new home even though I lost my rings. The house was just right. Dwain was a baby, and he had his own room. We were proud of that fact. I would rock him to sleep in a straight chair, and then I would ease up and put him in his bed. I would tiptoe back to my room. As soon as I got in bed and settled down, he would start crying. We ended up putting him in the bed with us so we could get some sleep. Remember, I was a first-time mother, and he didn't come with directions. He had slept in the room with us, so he soon learned he didn't want his new room by himself. We moved his baby bed in our room with us and he was okay.

We met all our neighbors on each side of us, and they didn't have any children. They helped us spoil Dwain. We enjoyed all our neighbors here. They were great.

I found a nice lady who lived behind us, and she kept Dwain when I was at work. She was an elderly lady with a large family, but her children were grown. She believed in teaching children to read and she read to Dwain. When we moved to Bainbridge, she gave him a set of books to read.

This set was called, The Sugar Creek Gang. Later on in life, I had the pleasure of giving this set of books to his two grandsons.

In Thomasville, after we bought our house, someone told me about a grocery store about a block off Main Street. The grocery store would let you phone in your grocery order for the day, and they would have a young boy deliver your groceries on bicycle. I never went to see this store, but I did call them and that is exactly what they did. Every morning, I would get my list ready for what I cooked for that day. The delivery boy would bring the groceries to me at the house. It was every day of the week except Sunday. We had to order on Saturday what we needed on Sunday. It was really great for me!

One day, the delivery boy came while I was visiting my neighbor. I had left the door open for the delivery boy. I wasn't gone very long, but when I got back, Dwain's money bank had been cracked open on my bedspread. All his money was gone except the pennies. Dwain never wanted to save any money after that day. The delivery boy got fired, and another one took his place. We kept on ordering groceries by the day. Every Monday when we got paid, we would pay for the groceries. Our bill was anywhere from seven to ten dollars each week. I never saw the inside of a grocery store until I was grown!

While living in Thomasville, I was working at Edwards Dry Cleaning and Fluff Dry. I was the cashier and sat in a little booth. There was only enough room in it for me. I had a window where I took money from the boys who delivered the dry cleaning and Fluff Dry to the customers' cars. I loved my job.

While working in Thomasville, I got into the spirit of things. Thomasville, Georgia, always had a rose show and parade. The businesses would sponsor a float in the parade. My boss asked me if I would ride on the float for the Laundry and Fluff Dry. He had recently added the Fluff Dry to the Laundry, and he wanted to advertise it. Of course, I said, "Yes."

They made the float and it had green carpet at one end and I was to sit in a chair on that end. My boss bought me a pretty blue dress to wear, and I was drinking a CocaCola and reading a magazine with packages of Fluff Dry clothes all around me. The Fluff Dry was used on the clothes that used to be ironed. The laundry would press the clothes, fold them, and wrap them in a package.

On the other end of the float, there were two washtubs, one for washing the clothes, and the other for rinsing. A line was stretched across the end of the float, and another girl was wringing out a sheet and hanging it on the line.

There was some dirt on the floor of the float, and she would drag the sheet in the dirt, trying to put it on the line to dry. It was funny. Our float won first place for the business float. The parade route was long. We rode at least two miles out to the building where they held the rose contest. Of course, you know what happened to me again; I got blistered. I looked the color of a red rose before we got where we were going. I really enjoyed my time at the laundry, and I worked there for two years when I found out I was pregnant with my second child.

Thomasville is the Rose City, and Vernon decided to get in the spirit of roses as well. He drove a truck for Nabisco delivering cookies. He left early in the morning, and he came in early in the afternoon. He loved working in the yards, and he had a beautiful rose garden. His boss man's wife came by one day and saw his roses. She asked him if she could cut one and enter it in the rose show. She chose one rose and named it a Peace Rose. She entered it in the show and the rose won first prize. It made us all very happy, especially Vernon. We were feeling proud. First prize for the float, and first prize for the rose. It was a great day! His boss man's wife kept the blue ribbon and the rose.

Vernon went to school at night to finish some courses he needed. While he was busy doing that, I joined a bowling league.

That's me on the bottom right

I would go and bowl and take Dwain with me. One night, a doctor's wife, who was bowling on another team, saw Dwain and asked me, "What's wrong with your little boy?"

At that time, Dwain was about four years old. I told the doctor's wife that I didn't know what was wrong with him. I had taken him to many doctors and they didn't know what it was. They told me he would grow out of it, but it didn't happen.

The lady said to me, "Do you mind if I make you an appointment with a doctor I know and let him look at him?"

I told her I would be delighted if she would.

She called me the next day and said, "You have an appointment next week."

We took Dwain to the appointment, and in one week, the doctor had him in the hospital, operating. They cut the artery in his neck and pushed his head up. Then they put a cast under his chin all the way to his knees. He had to stay in the body cast for six weeks. He learned to run and play around the house by bending over a bit and looking over his cast on his neck and head. It didn't seem to bother him.

The actual problem Dwain was operated on was called Rye Neck. After the six weeks were up, the doctor took the cast off, and

I dreaded it. He took a saw and cut the cast right off. Dwain's little head dangled all around. It was a good thing that I had quit my job at the cleaners when I found out I was pregnant because I was now dedicated to helping Dwain. It was my job to put him on the dining room table and turn his head from left to right and pull it to me at the same time. I had to do this ten times a day. This was not easy since I was pregnant with Jill. Don't you know that was a lot of fun?

After we did this for about two months, I had to take him to therapy in town. This brought on a little problem because I didn't drive. To make matters worse at this time, we had a stick shift car. Vernon loaded me up and headed for the country to teach me how to drive. I learned fast and did really good. The first time I parked in town, I thought I had done something great. Off to therapy we would go, and I must say all my efforts paid off.

I have been driving ever since that time. I just got a new license, and I am ninety-two years old! My son Dwain is a good-looking boy since we got his head straight.

We had some friends who worked for Nabisco. They attended the First Baptist Church in Thomasville, and they wanted us to go with them. We hadn't been to church since we got married and I was so glad they got us started with them. I was in my friend's Sunday school class. The first Sunday I attended, the teacher asked me to pray. Oh, what a mess I got myself into! It had been a long time since I said a prayer in front of someone.

Before I prayed, I said, "Lord, you got me into this, would you please get me out?"

I started praying just what the Lord put in my mind. I didn't do so badly, so I thought. The teacher didn't ask me to pray again. I soon left that class and started teaching four-year-olds.

Dwain was five years old on October 15, and Jill was born October 30, 1951. A girl, oh happy day! We were so excited to have a boy and a girl. Since I didn't have a job at this time, I decided to open a daycare center. I had three children from other families and two of my own. I charged one dollar a day per child. We really had a great time. All the children played good together and took a nap after lunch. I did too. I kept the children for two years.

Then things were interrupted. Vernon came home one Friday afternoon with a huge smile on his face.

I asked him, "What are you so happy about?"

He said, "What town do you like the most, Moultrie or Bainbridge?"

I asked, "Why?"

He said, "I just wanted to know. I hate to tell you this, but we have to move again. We have a choice between Moultrie and Bainbridge."

I asked, "Why are we moving this time?"

He said, "You will never guess what happened to me today."

I said, "Well, tell me and don't keep me guessing!"

Vernon said, "I got a promotion! I am now a salesman for Nabisco! I will no longer be a truck driver."

I was so excited for him. No one deserved that promotion more than Vernon. I gave him a big hug and told him how proud I was of him.

After all this sunk in, Vernon said, "If it's okay with you, I'd like to move to Bainbridge. I like it the best." (See map number 17.)

I told him that was okay with me. I knew I would need to find another place for my daycare children to go. I had been keeping three children for three years.

Chapter 31

Our Life Begins in Bainbridge, Georgia

We did move to Bainbridge in 1955. There was an air base located in Bainbridge at that time, so there was not a house to be found. We went to the First Baptist Church and met a lady by the name of Helen Simpson whom everyone called Ms. Helen. She was the secretary of the church and a wonderful person. While we were talking with Ms. Helen, the preacher came down to where we were and introduced himself. His name was James T. Burrell. He told us he was just reading a letter from the pastor from Thomasville. The pastor told Dr. Burrell to be on the lookout for us. We were good Sunday school teachers. It was true. I taught the four-year-olds and Vernon taught the primary boys in Thomasville. Well, you know what followed the first Sunday in Bainbridge? We joined the First Baptist Church and moved our letter from our Thomasville church to our new Bainbridge church.

I started teaching the four-year-olds in Sunday school and Training Union. I taught for twenty-five years. When all our children were through with going to their classes, I gave it up and joined a Sunday school class of my own, The Fannie McQuaig Sunday School Class. I am still a member of this class to this day.

Fannie McQuaig's Sunday School Class
at My Ninetieth Birthday Party

We introduced ourselves to Ms. Helen once again and told her we were looking for a place to live. She got on the phone and made a few calls and found us an apartment on West Street. It was a house that had an apartment with one on each side. One side was large and the other was very small. A man who worked for the post office across the street lived in the big side. His wife had left him, and he told us he would move over to the smaller side and let us have the big side. It was fine with us. Even the big side wasn't big enough for a family of four, but we made it okay.

The house had two big bedrooms and a kitchen and a bathroom. It had a potbelly stove in the middle of one of the bedrooms. It took a gallon of kerosene a day to keep us warm. We only had one car and Vernon needed it on his Nabisco route.

The two children, Dwain who was seven years old, and Jill who was two years of age, and I, had to walk two blocks every day to a gas station to get a gallon of kerosene.

We had been in the apartment about two weeks, and every night, we would smell something that would burn our eyes and it was horrible. Dwain would cover his head at night to keep from smelling the odor. We thought the smell was coming from a tree outside our bedroom window. We were getting ready to cut down the tree. Before we cut the tree down, I finally decided to go over to the neighbor and ask him what could smell so bad in my house.

He came over and looked and said, and I quote: "Vernon, don't light no cigarette. It will blow you up!"

What had happened was when the man moved to the small part of the house, he moved his gas heater with him and he stuck a piece of paper in the hole where the gas pipe had been. Every night and day, we were moving our bed back and forth so we could make it up and the paper over the hole had worked itself loose. Our apartment was full of gas fumes, and that was what smelled so bad and was making us all very sick. We took care of the hole and no more smell. Thank goodness the Lord took care of us. Needless to say, I got really tired of going to that gas station every day to get fuel for the potbelly stove. I decided I would get busy and start looking for another place to live.

Chapter 32

December 1955

I started looking in the newspaper for a house with three bedrooms. There were only two three-bedroom houses in the part of town that I wanted. I called the realtor and talked to him about those two.

He said, "One house is on Sims Street and the other house is on Lake Douglas Road."

The one on Sims Street was on a paved road and the one on Lake Douglas was a dirt road. Lake Douglas had very few houses on it and no trees. It looked very hot with the sun facing the front most of the day.

I told the realtor I would tell my husband about them, and we would get back with him when we were ready to look at them. Vernon didn't know anything about me looking for a house, and when he came home, I had to explain to him what I had done. We discussed it thoroughly and Vernon did not think we could afford a house. I told him it was getting cold in November, and I couldn't be trotting up and down that street every day to get fuel for that pot-belly stove, plus having to carry the children along as well. We talked quite a bit more, and I got my point across.

We looked at the house on Lake Douglas first, and when I walked in, the first thing I noticed was pine panel walls. The house had three bedrooms and none of the bedrooms were larger than the other two. It was just perfect. The kitchen was painted a pretty yellow over the pine panels. It had a small screened-in porch on the back and on the side of the house. The one on the side was off the living and dining room. We liked this house so much we never went to look at the other one.

It was several weeks before we could get the papers signed and all the things you have to do to get ready to move in. In the meantime, we enjoyed our apartment. There was a couple who lived about two houses down from the apartment and they had a son about the same age as Dwain. We became good friends with this couple. Their name was Johnny and Luther Bryant. She came to see me one day and told me she was expecting another baby. We got so excited. I told her I had some baby clothes she could have, and I would gather them up and wash them and get them ready. She left my house very happy. I kept busy gathering all the baby things that I had and was glad to get rid of them.

Days went by and I wasn't feeling so good for some reason. I decided I'd better go to the doctor and see why. I was so sick in the mornings. Well, lo and behold, I was pregnant too! I called my friend and asked her to come over because I had something to tell her.

When I told her my news, she said, "I guess I won't be getting any baby clothes, will I?"

Both boys were born in December. My boy was born December 23, 1955. He was named Vernon Thomas Shaw Jr. after his daddy and he was beautiful.

We finally moved into our new house in December 1955. We really liked it, and as I am writing this story, we have lived in this house for fifty-seven years.

1205 Lake Douglas Road in 2016

All my life, I moved from place to place at least eighteen times so I was so glad to call this house my home. This was a very big Christmas for us. Vernon bought a new car; so we had a new home, new car, and most important, a beautiful new baby all in a week's time. We loved all three.

I had mentioned before that I kept children while I was in Thomasville. I had been very close to a little boy named Larry. One of my friends from Thomasville called to tell me Larry had cancer and was very sick. I left Bainbridge to go to see Larry. I took some games, candy, and books. We spent the day together and had a great time. Larry died two weeks later. He was like my own child and that was so, so sad. It took me a little while to understand this, but I knew I had to move on because I had three children, a husband, and a new house to tend to.

Chapter 33

My First Child:
Joel Dwain Shaw

The Jack-in-the-Box costume that I made.

Dwain was starting school at Elcan King School about three blocks from our house. He became a crossing guard and loved it. He wore a uniform and stopped cars on a busy street. He was so good at this and kept that position for over two years.

Soon after we moved here, Dwain found a friend in the neighborhood. Children can always find friends before the adults can. This new friend's name was Wayne Godwin. He lived about two blocks from us. Wayne took me to meet his mother and she was so nice. She offered to take me any place I needed to go. I now had a very good friend name Hilda Godwin. Hilda Godwin and I became great friends throughout our life in Bainbridge. Years later, her husband passed away, and she moved to live near her son. Dwain and Wayne were inseparable all the years in school. Not only did they enjoy their school time together, they spent many hours together playing guitars and singing. They had formed a singing group with another friend, and they ended up entertaining all around town. They were really good and they played for free.

Dwain had tried his hand at football, but I think he was doing that for his dad. One day, the coach had asked Dwain if he really wanted to play football. Dwain confessed then and there that he didn't really want to play. The coach sent him home. Dwain knew in his heart he really wanted to play the guitar and you can see that's exactly what he did.

During this time, we had a little surprise news coming our way. I had not been feeling good, and I thought I better go and see the doctor. So I did and I got the shock of my life. He told me I was pregnant. What! I was forty years old, and Dwain was graduating from high school. Jill was going into junior high school and Vernie was in the fourth grade.

I just couldn't believe it! I kept this news from the kids for several months. Of course, I told Vernon and he was happy.

He said, "Maybe we will get that little girl all of us wanted."

One day, I came home from work and I wasn't feeling too good. Jill noticed it and said, "Mama what's the matter?"

I said, "Nothing, I am just tired today."

Jill didn't say anything else and went to practice piano. After awhile, Dwain came home and noticed me too.

He asked the same thing. "Mama, are you sick?"

I was really getting worried then and asked them, "Do I look that bad?"

Jill said, "I know something is wrong. Do you have cancer?"

Dwain asked that too. I knew then I had to tell them the truth.

I said, "Well, Mr. Smarty, if you really want to know, I'm going to have a baby in October."

Shocked and surprised, but happy, Dwain put his arms around my waist and swung me around and around. Jill was jumping up and down. It was just a great big happy moment for us. We were all waiting and praying for a baby girl.

On October 25, 1963, I went to the hospital, and I did have a little girl. We named her Tammy Gay because she was born smiling and a happy baby. Since I was a little girl, I had told my mama I wanted two boys and two girls. It took me a long time to accomplish it, but I did it at the age of forty, almost forty-one. I now had my four; two girls and two boys. We were a happy family of six.

When Dwain was in school, he belonged to a group that had to make a float for a parade. They were playing a team whose mascot was a tiger. They needed a big tiger to hang upside down on the float. Guess who made the tiger? He needed it, and you know mothers try to do anything for their children. This was a problem for me because I was expecting a baby any day now, and I wasn't sure I would be able to make that tiger. I told him I'd do the best I could.

I found a large piece of orange material in my cloth box. It was large enough to make a tiger. I got an old newspaper and cut me a pattern. When I got one that satisfied me, I cut it out and started sewing on it. I sewed it all together and left a place to put the stuffing. I had to leave it just as it was because I went to the hospital and had a beautiful baby girl. I was in the hospital for two weeks. It was left up to Dwain to finish the tiger. He had to stuff it and that he did. I never thought to ask him what he stuffed it with. He told me a group of his friends got together and finished it and it looked good on the float.

When I got home from the hospital, I was ready to put on some of my dresses that I could wear again after having the baby. I was very tired of maternity clothes. I started looking for my clothes that I had folded and put in a box in the closet. I started pulling dresses out of the box in the closet and every one I pulled out had black stripes on them. I looked like a tiger.

When Dwain came home from school, I said, "Dwain, what did your group stuff the tiger with?"

He said, "Mama we didn't know what to do, and I found a box of clothes in the closet and we stuffed him with those. We were running out of time, so we used the first thing we could find."

I said, "What did you use for the black stripes on the tiger?"

He said, "We used a few bottles of black shoe polish."

It was a relief because I thought that it was black paint. The shoe polish washed out of my clothes. Thank goodness! Oh to be a mother is never a dull moment!

Dwain went to Middle Georgia College for two years and then went to the University of Georgia. While in school, he was in ROTC, which was getting him ready to go and fight for the USA. It was exactly what happened. Dwain enlisted and made a twenty-year career in the army. Dwain retired as a Lieutenant Colonel, and when he left there, he went straight to work as Director of Information Services for the Medical College of Georgia Hospital and Clinics in Augusta, Georgia. He is now retired again and enjoying his passion of teaching photography at a college in Augusta. Dwain was married to his high school sweetheart, Betty Shellman Shaw for forty-three years. Betty had rheumatoid arthritis and left this world way too soon. Dwain has since remarried Leilani Nagel and they reside in Augusta, Georgia.

The following pictures are in loving memory of our Betty

Pictured above is Dwain and Betty's only child, Jennifer

Chapter 34

My Second Child Patricia Jill Shaw

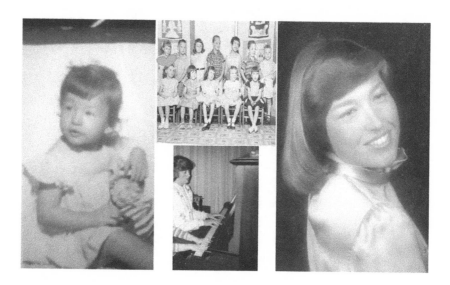

My second child and my first girl entered this world on October 30, 1951 in Thomasville, Georgia, one of the nicest surprises in my life. The night she was born was pretty rough. A friend of mine in Thomasville named Mary Helton took me and Dwain to a Halloween contest in downtown Thomasville. We had to walk with our children as they went around in a circle. They had to walk so the judges could see them. I had made a costume for him. He was a Jack-in-the-Box. Dwain won first place in his age group. Mary was walking with him because I was hurting and had to go and sit down. I tried to sit down and I couldn't sit. I hurt worse trying to sit. I had never had labor pains when Dwain was born, and I didn't know I was actually in labor. I told Mary we had to go home and we did go, very quickly. I went to bed.

About 3:00 a.m., I told Vernon to call Mary to come and get Dwain because it was time. I needed to go to the hospital. We thought we were going to have her in the car. We didn't have time to call the doctor. We just flew to the hospital. The nurse came out to the car to get me with a wheelchair after Vernon told them what was going on. The doctor fussed at me for not calling him. He didn't have time to prep. He gave me an epidural shot and Jill was born in twenty minutes. I slept through it all. When they woke me up, I had a little baby girl in my arms.

I really didn't think I could have girls because my sister had two boys and my mother had five boys. Oh, that was a happy day for me and Vernon. He wanted to name her Patricia, and I said I like Jill. I asked him if it would be okay to call her Jill. He said, "Yes!"

Jill just fit her to a T. We named her Patricia Jill. She was a good baby and a pretty bald-headed baby.

My friend Mary kept Dwain until I came home from the hospital. Mary and her husband didn't have any children, so they enjoyed keeping Dwain. When Dwain saw his baby sister, he was proud. We had a five-year-old and a brand-new baby.

When Jill was about three years old, Vernon and I went to Tifton to see his parents. We were going to take Mama Bessie to Augusta to visit with Frances, her daughter, and their family. Of course, Mama Bessie and Papa James were anxious to see our baby girl and Dwain. After traveling to Augusta on Saturday afternoon, the women decided we would go uptown in Augusta and shop around. I was holding Jill's hands as we walked along, looking at the things in the window of the shops and all of a sudden, I missed Jill. She had gotten away from me, and I didn't realize it. I was so scared. We were frantically looking up and down the street and in the stores, but we couldn't find her. We called the cops, and they came and helped us look.

I finally went in one big department store and I called her name. I heard her say "Mama," and I went to her. She was sitting on the counter where they have the cashier. They had all gathered around her talking to her. They had already called the cops to come and get her. I had her dressed so pretty that day. She had a purple dress and socks and ribbon in her hair, all just alike with white shoes. She was a doll. I asked her how she got in there.

She said, "Some woman asked me if I was lost and I told her I was. So she took me in this store and left me."

At the time this happened, I was eight months pregnant with Vernie, and I thought I was going to lose him. I was so scared. I was one happy person to see my little girl and she was okay. We didn't want to shop anymore so we went home.

Jill always had straight hair which was very pretty and very thick. All of her friends had curly hair. Jill decided she wanted her hair curled. I was used to giving home permanents to all my friends around, and I didn't think it would be any trouble giving her a permanent. She came home from school and we started on it.

First, I cut it and then I rolled it. Then, I put the solution on her hair to make it curl. After so many minutes, I took the rollers out and rinsed her hair with warm water. It was time to finish up with rinsing it again. It was a school night and I thought I'd finish in time to go to bed. Her hair was so thick, and I never counted on it being so hard to dry. We stayed up as late as we could and it was still wet. She went to bed and the next morning it was still wet. We combed it out and it was curly all over and wet and time to go to school. I told her she didn't have to go to school, but she didn't want to miss a day of school. She put a scarf over her hair and went to school and kept the scarf on all day long. She decided she didn't want curly hair anymore. I bought a solution to take the curls out and she has had straight hair ever since. Her hair is real pretty to me.

Jill joined the band in junior high and won many awards. She continued band in high school. She played clarinet and was very good. We had a Cocker Spaniel dog named Frisky. He loved Jill. He would follow her to school every day and stay under a shade tree until school ended. Frisky would follow Jill home. When she went to band practice after school, Frisky went too. The band director said the dog was present more than some of his band members!

Jill had a best friend named Sheryl Maxwell. They met in kindergarten. Sheryl was an only child. Her parents were non-verbal, nor could they hear. Sheryl used sign language with her parents and throughout the years at Sheryl's house, Jill learned sign language too.

One night, Jill was going to spend the night with Sheryl. Of course, Frisky went along as well. The girls were in junior high, and the school was a couple of blocks from Sheryl's house. They started to school one morning, and they didn't want Frisky to follow them, so they tied him to a chair on the back porch. As they started to school and got halfway there they heard a *click clack, click clack* noise. They looked around and here comes Frisky, chair and all. What a funny sight!

Our next door neighbor had six children: five boys and one girl. The girl was the same age as Jill and they became great friends. One day, Jill came in crying. I asked her why she was crying. Jill said that Kaye, her friend, was moving to Autaugaville, Alabama, near Montgomery. The family did move and Jill was so upset for a while. Kaye was friends with Sheryl too. After the family had been gone for a while, Sheryl and Jill got a wild hair to just drive to see her. The girls both played in the band, and they had a band concert in the downtown park.

After the concert was over, they were to go back to school. They decided to skip the rest of the school day and just drive over to Montgomery, Alabama, to see Kaye. Sheryl had a car so they left without telling me or her daddy. They didn't know Montgomery was so far, nor did they know the way. They didn't tell anybody where they were going because they thought they could just run over there and be back by the time school was out and nobody would know they had gone.

Sheryl's daddy came to my house every thirty minutes, wanting to know where Sheryl was. I would tell him each time he came that I would like to know where my daughter was too.

Her dad and I were so worried. We had no idea where they would go without letting us know. About six that evening, I heard a car in my drive. I looked out and there were two lost girls. Lord, I was so happy to see them that I couldn't even be mad at them.

They came in and told me that they took a trip to Montgomery, Alabama, to see Kaye and it took so long to get there, they only had time to visit with her for ten minutes. They knew they better get back home fast. They had seen snow coming back and were glad because we never had snow in our town. Sheryl didn't stay but a minute. I told her to get home and let her dad know she was okay.

At our house, we had an old upright piano that we had moved every time we moved. No one played it. It belonged to Vernon when he was a young boy, and he actually played it for his church in the country. One day, the football coach came to his house and asked Vernon if he would like to play football. The coach also asked his parents. They all agreed and he stopped playing the piano.

The piano sat for many years. When Jill was small, she would sit down and look at it and say, "I wish I could play." She picked out a few little songs by ear. When she was in the eighth grade, she had a friend that played.

This girl's name was Myra and her father was blind and he tuned pianos. Myra had taken lessons for years and was great. Her piano teacher told her she could teach someone if he wanted to. She was so thrilled and said, "I know who I want to teach. It will be Jill Shaw."

She asked Jill if she would like to take lessons, and of course, Jill was so excited, she said, "Yes, yes, yes!"

Myra charged fifty cents an hour, and Jill would babysit to make money to pay for her lessons. Jill loved to play. She stayed on the piano every extra moment she had. Our family was so proud that she could finally play her dad's piano. The piano is still sitting in our living room, and it still sounds good. It is probably ever bit one hundred years old. Every Christmas, we have a great time all sitting around singing and enjoying Jill's playing.

Jill finished high school in 1969. She had decisions to make about a college. She thought about this one and that one. Finally, she decided on a small college in Americus, Georgia. It is now Georgia Southwestern University. This college was closer to home. Jill never liked being away from home especially with a new baby sister to play with.

I will never forget the day we packed her up to leave for Americus. It was pouring rain. It rained all day, and when we arrived in Americus, we had to unload her suitcases and everything else in the rain.

I helped her to her dorm, and we met her roommate. After a week of this girl, Jill had had enough. She wanted to come home. This particular roommate had everything else on her mind except studies. If Jill had had a car, I do believe she would have come home!

We worked through this day by day until Jill met a new friend named Joan. Joan and Jill became friends and later became roommates. Joan had a car and brought Jill home for the weekend.

When I met Joan, I knew that Jill had met the right girl. We fell in love with her, and she became a part of the Shaw Family. Jill and Joan finished college together and moved to Cordele, Georgia, to begin teaching. To this day, they are best friends. Joan married Mike Wilson and Jill was her maid of honor at their wedding. They have two great sons who also teach. Jill enjoys being a part of their lives and her beautiful grandchildren's lives.

Jill moved to Valdosta, Georgia, where she continued teaching music. She received the honor of Teacher of the Year for one of her elementary schools, S.L. Mason in the Valdosta City School System. Ten years later, she received the Teacher of the Year for Lake Park Elementary School in Lake Park, Georgia. So much of Jill's life involved children. She was also chosen Teacher of the Year for Lowndes County Schools.

Needless to say, we were very proud of her. Jill retired from teaching and now lives with me in Bainbridge. She is my caregiver, and one of the loves of my life!

Chapter 35

My Third Child Vernon Thomas Shaw Jr.

Vernie's Sports Trophies

This little boy was good since the day he was born. He was a pretty baby. Vernon's boss man came over from Thomasville to see him and he said, "That's the prettiest baby I think I've ever seen."

He was almost a Christmas baby, born on December 23, 1955. He was named after his dad. Vernon Thomas Shaw Jr., but he was my second son. The reason he has his dad's name is I decided he might be my last son, and I wanted to have a Junior. The reason my first son Dwain did not get that name was because Vernon's mother, Mama Bessie, wanted to name him Joel. We did name his first name Joel, and I added the Dwain to it. Everyone was able to be involved in the naming of my first son.

When the children were growing up, we had a neighborhood full of children, and all of them played in an empty lot that was beside our house. It was a football field. The neighbors across the street had three children: Gene, Janice, and Everett Perkins. Next to them was a family with six children, and the empty lot next to our home soon had a house built that had six children.

My front yard turned into the football field. All the kids were in and out of the house all the time. Little Vernon became known as Vernie, which we still call him. Vernie was the smallest one of all, but he hung right in there with them. Everett Perkins was one of his best friends. The Perkins had a swimming pool in their backyard and all the kids enjoyed that.

The children attended Elcan King Elementary, which was only a few blocks from our house. It went from first grade to the sixth grade. All of the schools had PTA, and I tried to go to everyone they had. I received a letter from the school telling me to be sure and come to the meeting being held at Jones Wheat School. The school was having a contest to see how many mothers would be there for each school. I felt it was my duty to go, but I had a problem. I had an eight-month-old baby girl, and I was keeping Everett that afternoon.

I decided to go and take them with me. There were a lot of mothers there. I went and sat on the front row. I knew my kids would mind me and be very nice. The principal was very nice. He and his wife had no children. When he saw the baby in my arms, he took her in his arms and kept her with him through the entire program. She was loving it, and she was no trouble at all.

I can't say that for my two boys! They told me they had to go to the bathroom. I let them go with a little promise that they would be right back. They stayed a while longer than they needed to. They just happened to go by the principal's office to plunder a little bit. They pushed several buttons to see what would happen and a few lights would come on and off. It was so much fun! Then they mashed this button, and it was the fire alarm. The whole school was turned out. I knew what happened, and I knew who did it. The principal went to his office to see what had happened with my baby girl still in his arms. There sat two scared boys waiting for their punishment. The principal looked at them and told them he needed a practice alarm and sent them back to me. There were no more problems out of them. It was a very exciting afternoon. I finally got my baby girl back, but she didn't want to leave his arms.

Vernie and Everett passed on to junior high. Vernie liked to play football and Everett didn't so they sort of parted ways at school.

Vernie was quite a football player at Bainbridge High School. We had a game one night. My friend, Mell Beall, and I went to the game. It was my first game to go see. I didn't know too much about football. The game was going strong. It looked too rough for me. Vernie was running down the field and a big ole boy was chasing him. The boy tackled Vernie, and he fell on the ground and that big ole boy fell on top of him. The first thing I did without thinking was holler, "Get off my boy!" Well, I embarrassed him.

After the game was over, all the boys on the other team teased him, saying, "Get off my boy," and they were laughing at him. I sure wished I hadn't said it, but that is how mothers are. Needless to say, I didn't go back to another game. His dad went to every game because Vernon carried the yard markers up and down the field. It was his job to measure the yards to see if a team scored a first down. He was up close when Vernie played. Vernie kept playing football. I didn't go very much. I didn't want to see the players falling on him.

Vernie was a good boy, and he wanted a new pair of Sunday shoes. I saved my money, and I took him to Mr. Grollman's Shoe

Shop. Vernie looked around and found a good pair of black, shiny shoes. He wore them to Sunday school on Sunday morning and showed them to all his friends. When we came home from Sunday school, I told him to take them off and put them up so he could wear them again next Sunday.

He said, "Can I wear them to school one day?"

I told him no because he might lose them.

He went to school, and I didn't see him leave. He decided to wear the shoes to school. He was so proud of the shoes, and he wanted to show them off. While he was at school, I noticed his shoes were gone from the house, but I had hoped he had put them somewhere. When he came home from school, he looked so sad. He was about to cry.

I said, "Vernie, what is wrong?" I looked at him, and he had some tennis shoes on his feet.

I said, "Vernie where are your new shoes?"

He said, "Mama, I wanted to show everybody my new shoes. We had PE today, and I had to change. I left my shoes right by the bench we sit on, and they were not there when I went to get them. They were gone."

Someone had taken his shoes and left an old worn-out pair of tennis shoes in their place. Vernie and I both felt sick about it.

Vernie had a girlfriend in high school named Susan Gardner. They ended up getting married after high school. They married at Pine Forest Baptist Church. When it came time to leave to go on their honeymoon, some of his friends had really used a lot of shaving cream to decorate the car. When Vernie went to get in the car, he got some cream on his hand. He started slinging his hand and his wedding ring came right off his finger. They searched and searched for his ring, but they could not find it, so Vernie and Susan stayed home on their wedding night.

The next morning, Susan's dad and Vernie went back to the church and parked right where they had parked the day before. He started shaking his hand just as he had done the day before. He started looking right in the path where he had been slinging his hand

and he found his ring! They were so happy, and then they left on their honeymoon.

Vernie and Susan have had a great life! He is a maintenance mechanic at Shaw Industry, and Susan is the office manager for Dr. Leverette, a local dentist.

Chapter 36

My Last Girl and My Last Child: Tammy Gay Shaw Connell

I made the clown costume.

I told you about Tammy's birth in another part of my story. She was a beautiful baby, and of course, the love of this family I finally got my two boys and two girls. The Lord has truly been good to me. All the family spoiled her.

When Tammy was eighteen months old, I entered her into a baby contest. I made her a little light-green dress. She wore green socks, pretty white shoes, and a green bow in her hair. She wore panties that had ruffles all the way in the back. She was escorted onto the stage, holding some lady's hand. When the lady turned her hand loose, Tammy put on a show. She waved at everybody in the audience and did a little jig. She would turn around and around showing her ruffled panties. When her time was up, she didn't want to get off the stage. I had to sashay out on the stage and get her. I'm proud to say Tammy won first place in her age group. She also won first place in everyone's heart.

Tammy was very tiny, and as she started growing up, it was just fitting that she took dance lessons and gymnastics. She was very talented in dance and performed with her dance troupe around Bainbridge. Everyone loved her dances. Of course, as she started getting older, we took care of all routine things for her. I will never forget she was having trouble with her teeth, so I made an appointment with the dentist. She had already had several appointments in the past, and she was getting tired of going. I told her that this is the last one for a long time. All the dentist had to do was clean them and put fluoride on them. Well, off we went, and they took Tammy on to the back. I stayed in the waiting room. Pretty soon, Tammy came running out to me and said, "Mama, you were right. He cleaned them and fertilized them!" We have had some great laughs about that over the years.

Tammy was a happy-go-lucky girl. She would talk with anyone and had many friends. When she was in school, she always had a new friend that she would bring home to spend the night. I never knew who the girl would be, but they would go to her room. They would talk, laugh, and have a good time.

All through elementary school, I had trouble with her talking too much. Every report card would say "Talks too much." One day, Tammy's teacher hit her on the shoulder with a ruler. Tammy was very small and skinny. I know that ruler hurt her. I went to her principal and talked to him about what happened. I told the principal that from now on whenever she did something wrong to get hit like

146

that to call me and I would take care of it. I also told her if she deserved to be hit with a ruler to put the hit on her little behind where it was supposed to be. I took care of the problem, and she never got another report card with "Talks too much."

Tammy was the light of all of our lives. Jill was twelve years older than Tammy, and when Jill got old enough to date, her dates would come in the house and visit for a while before they left to go out. Tammy, who was about four or five years old, would head right to Jill and her date. She had a way with her dates. Tammy would get real close to Jill and try to talk her into letting her go with them on the date. It didn't work, but she kept trying. I do remember, one time, Jill did take her to a ballgame in the afternoon. In the middle of the game, Tammy had to go to the bathroom, so Jill took her to the outhouse! Jill didn't even think about the fact that Tammy had never been to a bathroom outside.

Tammy said, "I'm not going to the bathroom in that thing!" She was something else!

One night, Tammy was sleeping with me, and she wanted to talk. I was so sleepy, and I had talked enough. I told Tammy to go to sleep. She would stay quiet for a while, and then she would say, "Mama" and talk some more.

She did that several times, and finally I said to her, "Tammy if you say Mama one more time, I'm going to move you to your bed."

She got very quiet, and I thought I could go to sleep now. I was almost asleep and out of the quiet I hear, "Mrs. Shaw!"

Well, she didn't say Mama.

As Tammy got older, she had friends in and out of the house. Two of her best friends in high school were Kay Starling and Cathy Brown. Cathy's dad was a doctor, and her mother was a nurse. During the times Tammy and Cathy were friends, Cathy's parents got a divorce. Cathy's mother moved into a house across the street from us. Tammy and Cathy became even closer friends. Everywhere our family went, Cathy came along even on vacation.

One day, I went to Tifton to visit with Mama Bessie, Vernon's mother. She was in a nursing home. I was going to get her and take her to Moultrie, Georgia, to see some of her kinfolk. I took Tammy and Cathy with me. Mama Bessie and I were inside, talking to her niece. Tammy came in to get the keys to the car to open the trunk. She had a ball to play with. Next door to where we were visiting was a small wooded lot with a small path to a church. The church had a basketball court, and they wanted to play.

Mama Bessie, Papa James's niece, Inez, and I were visiting quite a while when Tammy came in and said, "Mama, we lost the keys to the car."

I got up and went to help find them. I stood there in the edge of the path, in the grass, and I prayed, "Dear Lord, please help me find the keys. I have to get Mama Bessie back to Tifton to the nursing home."

I walked a few steps and looked down, and there they lay. Thanks to Jesus for answering my prayers. I got Mama Bessie back to the nursing home on time and we left for home.

We stopped in Cairo and got some hamburgers. We got home safe and sound. Vernon was home when we got home and asked, "Why are you so late?"

I said, "We had a little excitement, and I'll tell you about it later." I had to get the girls to bed.

Since I had four children, I was having to buy things for the older three, and I was always putting things off for Tammy. I told Tammy her time would come. One day, we went by a store, and they had some pretty dresses in the window. Tammy opened the door of the shop and said, "My time has come." I went in with her, and she picked out four pretty dresses. She went home happy.

Tammy was always fun to be with. You never knew what she was up to. She enjoyed school, dance lessons, and gymnastics. She excelled in dance and her teacher wanted her to be her helper, and she did for a while.

I thought I heard Tammy say she wanted her bedroom decorated in all red. While she was at school, I went to work. I bought her a red-and-white bedspread and curtains in red and white. I bought some red throw rugs for the floor. I called the telephone company and they brought me a red telephone (that was before cell phones). I mean, I had a beautiful room! I had red lights in the room.

I couldn't wait for her and her friends to come home from school. She never came home without some girls with her. They walked in and went straight to her room. That's what she always did. She was so surprised! All of the girls loved it and had fun off it. She would say to the girls, "Come on home with me. We are going to the red light district!"

It was fun for a while, and she finally told me she didn't like red anymore. I changed it to a pretty blue room. She almost got her way every time. Love is all about that!

Tammy met this boy and fell in love, and she didn't want to go to college. She got a job at Shaw Industry and loved working there. She was good at her job at Shaw, and she won worker of the month. She got to park in a special parking place in the front of the building.

One day, she surprised me and asked if she could get married. She did not want a big wedding. She wanted to go to the courthouse. The groom's mom, dad, and I went with them. When they left the courthouse, I was going to take a picture of them. I'm not much of a photographer. I sent the picture off to be developed. When I saw them, all I had taken was their feet.

Tammy married Tommy Connell and continued working at Shaw until they closed out her part of the plant. The plant offered severance packages, and Tammy took the opportunity to go to Bainbridge College and she became a nurse. Vernon and I were so very proud of her. She had become a great nurse, and she had many opportunities to work in many different areas. She uses her talents with me now as my own personal nurse and caregiver. I love it.

One day, I picked up the town newspaper and there was an ad in the paper for a contest. It was getting close to Mother's Day and this was a contest to vote on the Mother of the Year. The paper wanted to hear from people about how special their mothers were. They had the contest for a young mother and an older mother. One day, I knew Tammy and Jill wanted me to read the paper as quickly as I could. I was just reading along. I turned the page, and there was a picture of me that said, "Mother of the Year."

I found out Tammy had written a piece for the paper about me. I just couldn't believe I won! I was so proud to think she would do that for me. I have the verse she wrote, and I want to share it in my story. What a blessing to have my special girl!

Mother of the Year

My Mother is my own personal spring, full of inspiration, love, and devotion. She's exceptional with many sides, and one of them will always be around for whomever comes to call.

She's a superhero—flying here and there, lending a helping hand.

She's a magician—pulling tricks out of her bag to everyone's surprise.

She's a seamstress—mending every family mishap.

She's a healer—healing with that special "Mommy medicine."

She's my best friend—holding my hand, lending an ear, always there for me.

She's the precious gem among our family's treasures. With God in her heart and a passion for life, she will try to Mother everyone. When I question her loyalty to all the world, she assures me that love gives love, a smile passes on a smile.

I pray every day that God leads me to be the beautiful individual she is.

Tammy Connell

Winners —

Mother of the Year essays

More than seventy-five letters were received from children honoring their mothers for *The Post-Searchlight's* Mother of the Year essay contest. The results were judged from two categories: children ages seventeen and above writing about their mothers and under seventeen. Here are the winners:

Evelyn Shaw

Mother of the Year
Over 17 category

By Tammy Connell

My mother is my own personal spring, full of inspiration, love and devotion. She's exceptional with many sides, and one of them will always be around for whomever comes to call.

She's a superhero—flying here and there, lending a helping hand.

She's a magician—pulling tricks out of her bag, to everyone's surprise.

She's a seamstress—mending every family mishap.

She's a healer—helping with that special "mommy medicine."

She's my best friend—holding my hand, lending a car, always there for me.

She's the precious gem among our family's treasures. With God in her heart and a passion for life, she will try to mother everyone. When I question her loyalty to all the world, she assures me that love gives love, a smile passes on a smile.

I pray every day that God leads me to be the beautiful individual she is.

Chapter 37

My Life as My Children Grew Up

So much of my life involved my children, but Vernon and I had a very rich life while our children were growing up, and as they moved on with their personal lives. I will tell you about our days together. I have lived in Bainbridge, Georgia (see map number 17) for sixty-nine years, and in our very same home at 1205 Lake Douglas Road. I have loved Bainbridge since day one.

I was welcomed by our neighbor Mary Ellen Strain who invited me to her house. She had a good friend at her house whom I met. This lady was Mell Slocomb. I thought she was so sweet. A few days later, Mell came to my door when I was home with the kids. Out of the blue, she invited us to go home with her and eat hamburgers. She lived about two blocks from us. We went with her.

Her house was a tiny little house on the corner of Lake Douglas Road. We joined together, her children and mine. We had a great time. She was a happy person, and I just fell in love with her.

Mell and I became best friends. Her husband was building a big brick home about a block from the smaller home, so that allowed us to remain close. Close we were, home-wise and friendship-wise, and we remained the best of friends until she died of cancer in April 5, 2004. I miss her to this day. She was the kind of friend you could tell anything to and she would listen.

Vernon joined an organization called the Masons and attended the Masonic Lodge. He really enjoyed it and became very involved. One of his responsibilities as a member was to coach new men who joined. They were not given any written laws of the Masons until joining; therefore, Vernon had to orally coach these men. Because he was gone most nights coaching, I was home with the kids. I decided I needed to help the family and get out of the house. I started looking for a job. Someone told me about selling Tupperware, a kitchen product. I became interested and started selling Tupperware. I would sell the product in the homes of people, mostly at night.

I worked selling Tupperware for two years. I won the Salesman of the District award, which included Tallahassee. As a bonus, I was sent to Orlando, Florida, for a chance to win best in the entire state. I traveled to Orlando with a girl from Albany. I drove and we had a great time. I did not win the best saleslady, but it was a great experience.

One day, they gave us a silver dollar and told us to spend it in any store or keep it. Each store selected some special items, and if you happened to buy one of those special items, it allowed you to get another prize when we got back to the meeting.

I moseyed around by myself, looking in on several stores. I had always wanted a salt-and-pepper shaker and a small can to put meat grease in. I went in to this one store, and they happened to have exactly what I wanted. I spent my silver dollar on it.

When I returned to our meeting, which had a huge crowd of people, they started by saying, "If you bought a so-and-so at this store, this is what you might get here."

They finally held up the very thing I bought, and I went down the aisle to get the present they were giving me. It was a nice coffee-pot. I just loved winning that prize.

We had a great time in Orlando. I sold Tupperware several more months, but I began looking for another job. I was tired of leaving my kids home at night.

Chapter 38

My Receptionist Days

One day, I went to my eye doctor for a check-up, and his receptionist was going to be quitting the job to get married. She told me about the job becoming available. I went the very next day and applied for that job and got it. For the next ten years, I worked for an optometrist, Dr. Sumner. He loved the eye business, but he also enjoyed building things. He was building the Glen Oaks Motel. When we didn't have eye customers, he would drive out to his motel and work.

One day, he decided to burn off some brush around the motel and the wind picked up and fire spread. It was spreading over to a neighbor's yard. He was working hard to contain that fire and it got away from him. A tragic thing happened. He fell into the fire and lost his life. That was an enormous shock to his family and to me.

Not only was it such sadness, but it was also a problem. This family had two businesses with no one to take charge. His wife, Lynette, and I worked closely to collect from the customers who owed him money. I actually worked for free to do this, and Lynette paid a babysitter to keep Tammy. His family needed the money to survive. I worked there until I could collect every cent I could.

Ms. Sumner sold the eye business to a new optometrist, Dr. Fred Shavey. I stayed and worked for Dr. Shavey for a while. In the meantime, I had put in an application at Bainbridge State Hospital. I wanted to work at a job that would allow me to draw a pension. I didn't have a penny to show for the years working with the doctors. The day he died, my paycheck stopped, and there was no pension.

Chapter 39

My State Job

Not long after applying for the state hospital job, I was called in for an interview. It was a three-to-eleven shift job. I wanted the night shift, but I told them I would take it.

I gave Dr. Shavey my resignation, and I went to work for the Bainbridge State Hospital. It was the best thing I ever did. I liked working with the children and adults who came in. I was in charge of a cottage that housed about twenty-five girls. I was responsible for their care. I worked in the cottage about one year, and then I was promoted to instructor.

This job was housed in a big building, and I had a room that was set up similar to a schoolroom. I was in charge of decorating the room with a bulletin board and materials suited to help the people learn life skills. I really liked this job. Before my promotion, I did end up working the night shift, and I never fell asleep at night like some of my coworkers.

One night, I lost my record of not falling asleep. I just could not hold my eyes open, and I fell asleep or sort of dozed off. I woke up very suddenly and looked at the clock. I jumped up and got all my people dressed and walked them to the dining room for breakfast. When we got over there, it wasn't open, and I wondered why. I looked at my watch again and we were one hour ahead of the time we were supposed to be there. I was so embarrassed. I never told anyone I did that. I can tell you it never happened again.

I was promoted to the instructor position soon after that incident, and it was a dayshift job. Thank goodness! I stayed in my new position, teaching away, until I turned sixty-five years old. At sixty-five, I did retire, and I had seventeen and one half years working for the state. I enjoy my pension to this very day!

In 1958, while living at Lake Douglas, our family was growing. We needed more space. We added a den to the back of our home.

One night, I was mixing up a cake and baking a ham. I was sitting in a chair with my shoes off, taking a little break. Vernon had been bird hunting all day, and he was lying across the bed taking a nap. The kids were outside doing sparkles. It was Christmas Eve.

As I was sitting in the chair, I thought I heard something crackle. I thought it was my ham in the oven. I just kept sitting there, and I heard it again. I thought, *I better check on that and I did.* I saw smoke coming from the corner of the kitchen. I quickly called the fire department and got Vernon up. I told him our house was on fire.

He said, "Call the fire department!"

I said, "I have!"

I was still working with Dr. Sumner, the optometrist, and he only lived about two blocks from us.

His wife said, "Bill, I believe Evelyn's house is on fire."

He walked down to our house to see about us. He took me and the children back home with him. I'll never forget Dwain was soaking wet. He had climbed a tree with a water hose trying to help put out that fire. When we got to Dr. Sumner's house, he gave Dwain a pair of his pants to wear and they made hot chocolate for all of us.

We stayed there awhile before we walked back down to our house. The city utility department would not let us turn the power on until they had time to inspect the house. All of us just went to bed and piled on covers to keep the kids warm. When the kids finally fell asleep, Santa Claus came and put the presents under the tree. The next morning, we had a cold Christmas morning with no power in the house. We looked at what Santa Claus brought them. Soon after that, we packed up and went to Tifton to Vernon's parents.

We stayed at Mama Bessie's and Papa James until they got our electricity back on. Since we built the new room on to the original house, the inspectors decided it was a wiring problem that caused the fire. We were very lucky. Here again, God was watching over our family and our home.

I've told you Vernie was a good boy, but I can't begin to tell you how helpful he was to me. I had to work to help make enough money for our family. I went to work at the Bainbridge State Hospital, and I wanted the night shift. They did not have a night shift position at the time I applied. I figured if I got my foot in the door, I would get a better chance to get the night shift. I really didn't know what I was going to do because Vernie was still in high school and playing football.

I got up very early in the morning and made breakfast for Vernon and sent him to work. He was a Nabisco salesman. They had to start early in the day. I would then let Vernie and Tammy sleep as long as I could. I would fix breakfast for them and help them get ready for school. I would take Vernie, Tammy, and our neighbor's daughter to school.

After I got the kids to school, I would cook supper for that night. My neighbor would pick Tammy up from school for me. When Vernie came home from school, he would take over for me and heat supper in the microwave. I would have a big pan of cornbread. This was always funny to me. Vernon and Vernie would always have one piece of bread left, and they would see who ended up with the last one.

After they ate, Vernon would go sit and watch television. Vernie would clean off the table and wash the dishes. He then would get his lessons, help Tammy with her lessons, and then help with bath time. Tammy hated bath time. She had long, thick, curly hair and that was a job just to brush her hair. He then put Tammy to bed. It was a job every night.

It wasn't long before I was promoted to the night shift. I would go to work from eleven to seven. It worked out so much better because I took back the chores that Vernie had been doing for me. He really helped me. Vernie was there for me every time I needed him. He can do most anything, and you can always depend on him. Vernon and I have always been proud of him.

Chapter 40

My Fun Night Adventure

Vernon and I had some friends who owned a small dress shop on Main Street beside the theater. The manager of the theater had advertised in the paper for someone to sit in this show at midnight all by themselves to see, *Let's Scare Jessica to Death*. The manager had built this up. He placed a coffin with a mannequin in the lobby of the theater. They wanted someone to sit through the movie all by themselves. It was supposed to be a very scary show.

One day, I started in Mr. and Mrs. Lanier's dress shop and I passed by the theater. The manager was standing out front. I stopped and asked him if he had had anyone to sit in the theater yet.

He told me, "No."

I said to him, "Put me down to do it."

The next night, I left work at 11:00 p.m. Then I took off to the theater. I re-dressed in the bathroom. I put on another pair of pants, a shirt, and a sweater. It was cold in the theater. I also put on a pretty brown hat. The manager took my picture while I was sitting in the theater.

He told me where to sit, and he took my picture with my mouth wide open and my eyes open like I was real scared. I was a little bit. I enjoyed the show very much.

When it was over, the manager asked me, "Was it scary?"

It was at times. I'd look behind me to see if anybody had slipped up. I didn't see a soul all night. I really enjoyed it by myself, and I didn't have to listen to my children upset me saying, "Mama, I've got to go to the bathroom," and I didn't have a big, heavy man with a big hat sitting right in front of me, keeping me from seeing the movie.

I forgot to tell you the rest of the advertisement. The manager posted in the ad that they would pay $25 for a person to stay all night. When it was over, the manager came up to me and handed me my $25. He thanked me for doing it and said, "You can go home now." I thanked him for the easiest money I had ever made.

This is the article and picture of me looking so "scared."

Let's Scare

Jessica to Death

The Martin Theatre in Bainbridge now brings to the screen the ultimate suspense thriller of the decade — Let's Scare Jessica To Death. Every minute is 60 seconds of scare suspense!

In a contest held by the Martin Theatre Mrs. Vernon Shaw of Bainbridge was selected to be the unlucky lady to view an advance private showing of the film at 12:00 midnight—all alone. Mrs. Shaw, now known as Shaky Shaw, did manage to force herself to sit through this horrific suspense thriller and received $25.00 for her bravery from the management of the Martin Theatre. Seated below in the picture is Mrs. Shaw as she watched the picture, all alone, the scare sensation—Let's Scare Jessica To Death.

When asked to comment on the picture, Mrs. Shaw just stared and with trembling lips kept repeating, Jessica, Jessica, Jessica. Needless to say, she had no fingernails. For thrilling, suspenseful excitement, don't you dare miss, Let's Scare

Jessica To Death showing Thursday, Friday, and Saturday at the Martin Theatre in Bainbridge. Don't see it alone, and be careful with whom you see it. No advance in prices.

Be sure to see Jessica in her casket on display in the lobby of the Martin Theatre. Casket furnished by The Cox Funeral Home and the mannequin furnished by Laniers of Bainbridge.

ADV.

Easy money?

Do you want to make $25.00?

The Martin Theatre would like to have some young lady over 21 to see alone at midnight their feature picture, Let's scare Jessica to Death. You will be the only one in the theatre other than the operator for this midnight screening. Watch The Post- Searchlight for the date of Let's Scare Jessica To Death.

If interested contact the manager of the Martin Theatre . . .

Chapter 41

Friends

Mell

Me, Essie, and JB

Vernon and I had so many good friends, but two special couples were Dorothy and Roger Beall and JB and Essie Walters.

We were invited to go and spend the weekend at the beach with some friends who had a house at Santa Rosa Beach. We arrived there late in the afternoon. We ate dinner and sat round and talked until late. The next morning, we were eating breakfast and someone knocked at the door. Vernon opened the door and it was a little boy about nine years old.

The little boy said, "Please come help my little sister. She is in the deep water and she can't get back."

Vernon and Roger ran down the beach and saw her up to her neck in water. It was too far out for them to go in after her. They kept their eyes on her, and she looked like she was floating, but she wasn't getting any closer.

We sent the little boy back to our cottage to get a rope and to tell Roger's wife to call the Coast Guard. The rope the little boy brought back was not long enough to reach her. Vernon and Roger went into the water as far as they could go and continued to watch her. As they stood there in the water about thirty minutes, they noticed the tide

164

was coming in. They stayed in place and when she got close enough, they got her out of the water and carried her to shore. They laid the girl on our jackets and shirts. The Coast Guard got there just as Vernon got her onto the sand.

The children's mother had gone to a beach with only two houses nearby and she could not swim. We asked the mother if we could carry her to the hospital and she told us she would take her. She thanked Vernon and Roger for saving her little girl. We called the hospital later that day, and she was not registered. She was breathing and alive while with us. We only hope she was doing fine. We will never understand why a mother who couldn't swim would take her children to this part of the beach. There were only two houses on this part of the beach and no one lived there. We just happened to be visiting for the weekend. That part of the beach was under construction.

After spending all of Saturday morning helping save a child's life, we decided to go to Panama City and look around the town.

There was a lot of traffic from Santa Rosa Beach to Panama City Beach. I dressed up more than usual to ride over there. My hair didn't begin to do any way to suit me. I had brought my wig with me, so I decided to wear my wig in case we decided to go anywhere. It looked better than my hair. I thought I looked pretty good with my wig on.

Panama City had an amusement park on the edge of town.

We stopped there first. It was like a circus. It had a tilt-a-whirl and a ferris wheel, a merry-go-round, and lots more. Dorothy, Roger's first wife, and I were trying to decide which ride we wanted to ride first.

Roger told us, "You can ride anything y'all want, but I'm not going with you."

Vernon said, "I'm not riding those things either."

Dorothy and I left them standing there and we started to the roller coaster. We got on and got square in the seat and that roller coaster went straight up! When you go up, you got to come down!

We were scared to death! It looked like we were going straight down on our head. It was so fast the wind blew my wig off, and I never missed it until we got off.

Dorothy and I started looking for Roger and Vernon and she never said a word to me about my hair. We were still looking for Roger and Vernon, and I never thought about my hair. It was the same color as the wig and it was messed up. Dorothy's hair got messed up on the ride too. I never said anything to her about her hair either. We were just concerned to find the guys. After walking around a bit, we saw them at the shooting gallery trying to win us a Teddy bear.

Vernon looked at me and said, "What has happened to your hair?"

I said, "What's the matter with my hair?"

He laughed and said, "It's a mess!"

I said, "If you had been in the wind that I had, you would have lost your hair too."

Then I realized my wig was in another world. I found a comb and combed my hair the best I could. I made a promise to myself that I would never get on another roller coaster, and I would never wear someone else's hair.

Chapter 42

Life on Spring Creek
"A Little Bit of Heaven"

My daughter-in-law told us about a lot on the lake right beside her aunt's. She had heard us talking about how we would like to have a place on the lake. We went to see it and bought two lots. We bought a mobile home and put it on one of the lots. We fixed it up and put a screen porch all the way across the back and we had a nice cool place to sit.

We enjoyed it so much! Later on, we added a dock. We loved to fish, so we went down to the dock every chance we got.

I had my special place on the dock. It was on the left side in the corner. Every time I put a fishing line in the water, I caught a fish, but they were not very big. Vernon would fish on the right side in the corner and he used a rod and reel. He didn't get as many fish as I did.

We took our daughter Jill to the lake with us. She loves to fish. We would all get in our special places. Vernon was sitting with his rod and reel, and Jill and I used an old fashioned fishing pole.

Vernon always wore a hat when he was down there because it was so hot. He was fishing away and he had a strike. He pulled really hard and his line went over his head. We started looking around for his fish, and we couldn't find it. Jill started laughing so hard. She saw the tail of a fish flapping out of the back of her dad's hat. The fish had landed in Vernon's hat. We have laughed about that for many years.

Our family really enjoyed our lake place. It was just a place we could go and relax and enjoy life as we were getting older and the children were grown and living their own lives. We were unable to keep the grass cut and keep it in good condition. The lake lot was deep and to get to the dock from the mobile home, we would drive down to the dock.

One day, we took friends down to the dock and it had really been raining a day or two before. It was muddy. We were taking our friends out to dinner after we showed them our place. They wanted to see the water, so we got out and went to look at the water and it was so pretty. We made the long walk back to the car and got ready to go and the car was stuck in the mud.

I got out of the car and opened the trunk to get some newspaper to put under the wheels in the back of the car. Vernon thought I was through, and he started the car. It slung mud all over me, and it was even dripping from my nose! I couldn't see at all. It had covered my glasses. My clothes were covered with mud and we were on our way to the restaurant to eat. We drove back to the mobile home, and I got some towels and tried to get the mud off as best as I could. It did not come out of my hair very well.

We went on to eat and found a table close to a wall. I sat with my face to the wall so nobody could see me. Every time Vernon and our friends, Zelda and her husband, LeDonne, looked at me, they would start laughing and I laughed with them. We had a very exciting afternoon.

Our family had many good times at the lake. Vernon got sick and couldn't walk to the dock anymore and my children didn't want me to drive anymore. They said I was getting too old (ha!). I did what they told me.

The place at the lake sat there for a year or so, and one day, somebody asked if I would sell it and I did. I'm sorry I did because my family could really enjoy it now.

Me and Vernon always loved being at the lake. Here we are sharing a special time together.

Chapter 43

Our Shrine Club Days

Vernon wasn't happy with just being a Mason. He had to go and join the Shriners. I didn't mind him joining these clubs because they are good organizations. Before you can become a Shriner, you have to be a Mason.

The Shriner's organization helps crippled children. They have a Shriner's Hospital in Tampa, Florida. Vernon drove many crippled children and their parents in the Shriner's van to Tampa.

Vernon took me on many occasions and we would explore all the buildings. It is amazing what they do. If a child needs an artificial arm or leg or anything, the hospital can do it. If they need braces, they can do it. All of it is free for the family. The Shiners raise money to support the hospitals. The Shriners support burn centers as well.

The Shriners have a chain of command with many different officers. Vernon got a call from a friend who was in a very high officer position. This position is called Potentate.

He asked Vernon if he wanted to be on the Divan. This is a position that would give you the chance to become Potentate. It takes ten years to make it to that position. Vernon told him he didn't think he would do it because his wife was sick a lot. When Vernon told me what his friend had asked and what he had told him, I told Vernon, "Call him right back and tell him you will take it."

I knew he wanted to do that very badly. He accepted the offer and they put him on the Divan, and he worked his way to the top in the nine years we had to get there. Those nine years were so much fun.

We traveled to so many places in the United States. We got to see Los Angeles, Las Vegas, New Orleans, and Niagara Falls. We even went to Canada and the outskirts of New York City. I just can't remember all of them, but I'm glad we got to go to all the places we did. Because he accepted the Divan position when he did, Vernon was Potentate in 1989.

We made it to the top in nine years because one of the Divan members had to move, so that bumped Vernon up a year. He became Hasan Temple Potentate in the Albany, Georgia district and I became the first lady.

Albany is sixty miles from Bainbridge, so we were up and down the road a quite a bit. The Shriners had a ladies' auxiliary called the Ladies of Nassau.

When we went to those meetings, we had to wear long evening dresses. One night, Ms. Essie and I had to go to a meeting by ourselves. The other ladies could not make it that particular night. I didn't know I was driving my car that night, so I did not gas up on the way to Albany. I noticed the tank was nearly empty, and I told Ms. Essie not to let me leave Albany without getting some gas.

We drove as far as Newton, a little town between Albany and Bainbridge. It had very few stores and one liquor store. Everything was closed because it was eleven at night. I looked at Ms. Essie and I said, "What are we going to do? I'm sitting on empty."

We spotted one place open, but we didn't want to go in because it was a juke joint. I knew that it would be full of men and it was. I had on a long red evening dress, and I thought I looked pretty good, but I didn't know what I was getting into. I told her to stay in the car and if I didn't come back soon, come see about me.

I walked in the joint and everybody stood still and stared at me. They didn't say a word. They knew I was out of place.

I said, "Hello, gentlemen. I'm a lady in distress. I'm trying to get to Bainbridge, and I'm out of gas. Could any of you gentlemen help me?"

I was very surprised at how nice they were. The man behind the counter told me he had a friend who owned a gas station and he would call him for me.

I waited and he called, but the line was busy, so I stood there talking to everybody until he called him again. This time, his buddy answered the phone, and he asked him if he would come to his station.

I thanked everybody and said, "Good night."

I went outside and got in the car and Ms. Essie said, "Gee, I was fixing to come inside and see about you."

I told her we were okay, and one of the men would lead us to a gas station in his car. His buddy came out and said, "Hello, ladies, how much gas do you want tonight?"

I said, "Please fill it." I thought he deserved to sell a whole tank for coming out to our rescue.

In the meantime, I realized, *Oh my gosh, I don't have any money!* I'm telling this man to fill it up, but I don't have any money.

I asked Essie, "Do you have any money?"

Thank goodness she had a twenty-dollar bill. During those days, you could fill up your tank with money left over. I told him to keep the change. We thanked him and we were on our way back, home safe and sound.

Of course, we had to explain this to our husbands. I paid Essie her twenty dollars back the very next day. Wow, what an adventure!

Being a first lady for a year and with Vernon a Potentate was a lot of fun. We got to go places we would have never gone. Every Potentate gets to pick a state to go to for their convention. Vernon picked Toronto, Canada. We had a big van that had room on top for our suitcase. There was a ladder on the back of the van to help with loading and unloading. The van was so nice and big, we could sleep in it if we wanted to.

The secretary of the Hasan Temple in Albany and his wife went with us. Most of the people attending the convention from Albany flew, but we decided to drive. Rufus, the secretary, had to carry so much for the meeting that we decided we would drive to carry everything.

The trip was great! We saw so much of the countryside and it was beautiful! We would stop along the way and get ice-cream cones to enjoy and cool us off. When we arrived in Toronto, we had reservations at this hotel called The Royal York Hotel. It was the oldest hotel in Canada.

When we started to unload our suitcases and take them to our rooms, I could tell it was old. The rooms had no place to hang your clothes and one bed for two people. They gave us the key to the room. We settled in to rest awhile. I had to go back to the van for something I had forgotten, and I locked the room door going out.

When I came back, I forgot our room number. I made a mistake and unlocked the door across the room from ours and the door opened. There sat a man and his son. I excused myself and closed the door. At that point, I found out every key in the hotel would unlock every door in the hotel. I then realized it definitely was an old hotel.

While the men were meeting, all the ladies had a great time checking the town out. Everything was so pretty!

There's a certain order or steps in the Shrine Organization. Each man who is appointed in these steps becomes a member of the Divan. The goal is to make it to Potentate, and it takes ten years. The ladies of the Divan's role are to take care of the first lady. The first lady is the Potentate's wife. At this time, it just happened to be me.

The ladies on the Divan really did take care of me. We went all over Toronto and saw so many pretty things. There was one thing that amazed me. There was a building with a tower, and it was so high it looked like it was in the clouds.

On top of the tower, it looked to me like there was a big room.

The Divan ladies asked me, "Do you like that?"

I said, "Yes, I do."

One of the ladies said, "Well, that's where we are taking you to lunch."

I said, "What do you mean, is there really a place to eat up there?"

I had never heard of anything like that. Off we went up the elevator, and it was bigger on the inside than I thought. It was a nice ride to the top, and when we stepped out, we were in the dining room. You can't imagine how pretty it was. We had great food and great service. After we ate, I gave the ladies a gift. This is customary of the first lady. After our nice lunch, we spent some time looking out the windows. We could see all over Toronto. We finally rode on the elevator back down, and I was very happy to get my feet back on the ground!

The Toronto Shrine Club was very nice to all of us that attended the convention. The time at the convention was so much fun. Before we knew it, it was time to head for home. Jean and Rufus Johnson, Vernon, and I drove together. When we left Toronto, we took our time going home. We drove to New York and went sightseeing. We were so tired from that, we headed south. When we got to Albany, Jean and Rufus were glad to be home. Vernon and I were glad to head home to Bainbridge. It was so nice to get to go on a trip like that.

When Vernon was put on the Divan, one thing that was customary was to host a party at your home. The people on the Divan needed to have time to get acquainted. The Divan members were coming from different towns. After the party, everyone goes to the Shrine Club for dinner. We had a big party at our house. We had about seventy-five people, and our house was packed.

One member from Tifton came late and asked me if I had a room to change his clothes. I told him yes, but before I could get to the room and show him where it was, another girl took it upon herself to take him before I could explain to them about the door. She had already shut the door. We had had problems with the bedroom door, and if it is shut, it locks. Our Divan member was now locked in our bedroom. He was creative and climbed out the window. Over the years, we have had some good laughs about this.

Our Divan friend teased me and said, "You just wanted to keep me." All in all, our party was a big success.

Thank goodness! I had worked so hard to make it a good party. I even made all the hors d'oeuvres.

Our shrine times were so much fun. We got so close to all the people on the Divan. One time, we went to a party at one of the Divan's house. I heard all about this man's special lemonade. I couldn't wait to try it. One of the other Divan's member's wives was also looking for this lemonade. We found it! It was the best lemonade! My friend, Avie, said the same thing.

We kept drinking it glass after glass. Vernon noticed it. He said, "You better not drink too much. It might make you sick."

We had one last glass and headed to our restaurant for dinner. Vernon asked me if I was all right. I was feeling a little dizzy, but I was okay. When we got to the restaurant, I felt a little different but I didn't say anything.

When everyone got there and we ordered our food, my friend Avie said, "Let's go to the bathroom." We went as quickly as we could. We were laughing and giggling in ways we would have never done.

When we got inside, Avie said, "Do you feel funny?"

I said, "I sure do feel silly!"

She asked me, "Do you think someone played a trick on us? Do you think the lemonade was spiked?"

I told her I thought they did, and we fell for it hook, line, and sinker! I had never had any whiskey before.

I told Avie, "We better get back to the table before we fall." I told her we should hold on to each other.

When we got back to the table, we agreed not to say a word so the joke would be on them. After the party, we found out that they did do this to all the new Divans' wives. That lemonade was sure good! It was the first time I had ever been drunk and the last!

Being a Shriner was so much fun! We got to travel and see so many places and things we would never have seen had we not been a Shriner. It took Vernon nine years to become the Potentate and that was a year-long celebration.

Chapter 44

The Potentate's Ball

When we got to the top, The Hasan Temple had a two-day cele-bration for the Potentate. On the Friday night, the Potentate gets to choose a theme party. On Saturday night, they have the Potentate's Ball based on their individual theme.

On Friday night, our theme party was, "On the Big Top," a circus name. Most everyone at the party was in costume. Vernon was the circus master, dressed in white pants, a red-and-white striped coat, and a red-and-white hat.

We hired a magician to entertain us after dinner. Everyone loved the party, and we heard about it for months after.

Vernon was a Nabisco salesman so we did a play on words. I decorated each table with Ritz Cracker Cans filled with butter cookies in a floral arrangement. The butter cookies were turned into ceramic models. I made the cookies out of dough and water. The cans decorated all of the tables.

We had top hats everywhere with small lights twinkling on the outline of the hats. They rolled out the red carpet for us to walk down.

At the time of the ball, I had a severe knee problem. I walked down the carpet, but they were nice enough to have a high chair in front so that I could sit down.

Vernon stood beside me. Each and every Divan member and past Potentates came down the red carpet and would greet Vernon and me with either a handshake or a kiss. There was certainly a lot of hugging. It was such a special night for us. Vernon and I were presented gifts from the Past Potentates. All of our children were there and they were introduced as well. Dwain, our oldest son, stood up by Vernon to present a gift to Vernon from all the children. It was the most beautiful diamond ring with a Shrine emblem around it. Vernon was so proud of it. After the presentation of the gifts, we were escorted to our table.

After that was over, the band started playing, and Vernon and I were to be the first couple to dance, and I hobbled out there. We danced and soon the dance floor was full. The dance continued until midnight. After the dancing, the members of the Temple served us breakfast. We were so tired after such a wonderful night. We headed to rest at our hotel.

On Sunday morning, they checked me into the hospital to prepare for knee replacement surgery on Monday morning. I stayed in the hospital a week, then I had to go to Bainbridge to begin the hard part of the surgery. I had to exercise my knee every day to try to work on getting it to bend. It was not fun. I spent the next four weeks working on my knee. Finally, I began to walk fairly well.

Vernon had been traveling by himself as Potentate until I got well. After I got well, I started traveling with him. It was so much fun to visit each chapter and swear in all of the officers for that chapter. We would also be treated to the best food.

The life of the Potentate is very short. He only had one year to attend many events before he had to give up being Potentate.

One of the special times we had was to host a Shrine Parade in Bainbridge. All the Shrine units from different towns would meet here and take part in our parade. Some of the units included a band from Blakely. They could really strut and it was so fun to watch a hillbilly band from Fitzgerald unit. They dressed in old hillbilly clothes with funny hats. They had this big old dog and when you got close to their bandwagon, the dog would raise his leg and wet on you! I got a dose of that one time.

Bainbridge had a banjo unit. There were about twelve Shriners, and they would march and play their banjos.

The parade was a highlight, and then everyone would eat, meet, and head for home.

Some of the responsibilities of being Potentate were to attend weddings, funerals, and visit the sick. I went with Vernon wherever he went. Our year passed very fast, but it was such a great part of our life. We really enjoyed it, and when it was over, we were happy to stay at home and rest awhile.

Chapter 45

My Mother's Life after Daddy

I'd like to tell you about Mama's life after my dad passed away. My mother was only forty years old when Daddy died, and she was left with three boys to raise. I've told you about the boys, but I want to continue by telling you what happened to my mother.

One day, she was reading the paper and came across an ad that caught her attention. The man was advertising for a friend. The ad looked good to mother. The man was retired from the railroad, and he lived in Warm Springs, Georgia. He was a guard at The Little White House. Mama liked what she read and answered the ad. He answered her and asked if he could come to see her.

She told him, "Yes."

He did come to see her, and Mother thought he was a very nice man. He looked nice too. He had beautiful snowy white hair. I was home at that time, and I really liked him too. They ended up courting for several months, and he asked her if she would marry him, and she said yes!

We found ourselves getting ready for a wedding. My sister Lottie came home. Lottie and I fixed up the church. They married at the First Baptist Church in Fernandina Beach, Florida. I was mother's matron of honor, and Billy had his son, Bill Greenwood, as his best man.

Billy had four children, and Mama had six children, but they were all grown.

After the wedding, they ended up going to Warm Springs to his home. My mother had never seen his house, and she was pleased.

Bill was very good to Mother, and I think she was the happiest I had ever seen her.

Mama and Papa Billy

Me, Mama, and Papa
Billy Greenwood

We ended up visiting them in Warm Springs, and Billy was a wonderful granddaddy to our children. He was so good to let the children go with him to work and see all the places Roosevelt lived.

Little White House in Warm Springs, Georgia and Papa Billy

He let Vernie sit in the car that Roosevelt drove. He let Jill sit on his bed. He worked the night shift and would let them tag along with him for a while. They loved going to Warm Springs to visit Papa Billy and Grandma Greenwood. We really all loved Billy, especially since he treated my mother so good.

They were married several years, and Billy became very sick. He was diagnosed with cancer. Mama and Billy were so devoted to each other when he had to go in the hospital. She stayed by his side night and day until he passed away.

After Billy passed away, Mother was in Warm Springs all by herself. It was very hard because Mother didn't drive. Warm Springs did not have a grocery store. She was having to get her neighbor to take her to a grocery store in the next town every week to get the things she needed. This got old very quickly and expensive. After a while, Mother decided she would go back home to Fernandina.

Fernandina Beach, Florida, is about forty miles from Jacksonville and where her three boys lived. They were happy to have her come home. She had the boys looking for a house she could buy. In several weeks, they had a nice house close to town. Mother sold the house in Warm Springs. The boys came up with a truck and loaded everything she owned and took her home. The whole family was happy to get her back home so they could visit with her more. Mother didn't live at the beach, but she was about a mile from it. Over the years, my family would drive from Bainbridge and visit with her.

One night, we drove to the beach, and at that time people could drive on the beach. We drove down the beach, and we saw this big turtle. I mean it was big! This big turtle was digging a hole in the sand. We stopped pretty close to the turtle and watched to see what she was going to do when she got the hole dug as deep and wide as she wanted. She sat down over the hole, and eggs came piling out of her. There must have been at least fifty. After laying the eggs, she covered the hole and crawled back to the water. It was the neatest thing for all of us to see.

I remember another time we went to visit Mama, Vernon, and my two brothers went seining for fish. They would take a net and wade out deep in the water and throw it. They would then drag the net back to shore and get the fish out of it and put them in a big tub.

My brother lived behind my mother. While the men were fishing, the girls, Mother and I, and my sisters-in-law all went to Jacksonville to shop. We came back tired and went to bed early. Vernon and my brother, James, carried the tub of fish to James's house. June, his wife, was also asleep. She was tired from the shopping trip too. The boys played a trick on both of us. Vernon came back to Mother's and found me asleep. He woke me up and told me June wanted to see me.

I said, "What does she want? I just saw her today." I got up and went to see June.

In the meantime, James told June, "Get up. Evelyn is coming over."

She said, "What for?"

She got up, and I was over there. I looked at her, and she looked at me. We knew then we had been tricked.

We looked down, and there was a big tub of fish. They wanted us to help clean the fish. We all went to work. June had never been around a fish in her life, but she was broken in that night. We all had fun. About daylight, we fried fish and had a good breakfast.

Chapter 46

Post-Potentate Shrine Time

Vernon and I had been so busy with the Shrine activities. We became accustomed to being on-the-go. When our Potentate year was over, we were not ones to just sit around. Vernon played golf, and he loved it.

One day, while he was playing, the manager of the Pines Golf Club asked Vernon if he would like to manage the club. It was great because it gave Vernon something to do. He had a job. The problem with the job was it did not include me.

I took it upon myself to go to the club with him. I helped him keep the clubhouse nice and clean. Some days I stayed home so I could have some well-deserved rest days because, after all, I was retired. I always enjoyed reading, sewing, and scrapbooking. I have made scrapbooks for most of my children and grandchildren.

I also loved cooking and making homemade jelly and pickles. One thing I've cooked throughout my years for our family is a sour cream pound cake.

Everyone loves it. My daughter, Jill, told me she could not ever remember coming home from college or teaching without my good ole pound cake sitting on the bar. Yum! I guess I've cooked a many of them in my years.

I also enjoyed making mayhaw jelly. It has been given to many a family and friend over the years. Each year in May, the mayhaw berries can be found. They grow on a tree in wet soil. The berry itself is not good to eat, but the juice from the berries taste great! You shake the berries out of the tree onto a tarp or anything that can collect them. I would take the berries home and wash them good. I removed all the trash and washed the berries until they were clean.

I froze the berries until I found time to make the jelly. When the time came, I boiled the berries and got the juice. I would then add Sure-Jell and sugar. The berries would end up as a beautiful jar of mayhaw jelly. It is the best jelly you have *ever* tasted!

Now that I am much older, I have gotten some help. My daughters help me. Jill now buys the mayhaws at the Farmer's Market, and the girls will help. I wanted someone to learn how to make it so we could carry on the tradition when I'm too feeble to make it. The mayhaw jelly will be part of this family forever!

Another treat my family has enjoyed is homemade sweet cucumber pickles. We like using the pickles for all our salads, potato, tuna, chicken, and egg salads. It adds such a great taste.

Well, you can see I didn't have trouble staying busy. In fact, there was not enough hours in a day to do all the things I wanted to do. Vernon was working at the golf course for over eight years. After the course closed in the evening, it was still light enough that he could play a round of golf. I would join him, and we would play together. Vernon was a very good player, and he was a good teacher. I enjoyed playing. He taught me well. I really miss playing now that I'm much older.

Now that our Shrine traveling days were over, every now and then we would want to get up and go some more. Jill had the summers free, and so we would take off somewhere. One of my favorite places was Branson, Missouri. We loved music so we couldn't wait to hear some of the entertainers. We had so much fun.

We stayed across the street from the Lawrence Welk Theater. We had tickets to see JoAnn Castle and the Lennon Sisters.

Wouldn't you know it that the night we went to see JoAnn Castle, she was sick! We never got to hear her play that piano. It was still a fabulous show.

One of my favorite shows was a breakfast show. The singers served us breakfast in their pajamas. After breakfast their show was *Music through the Ages*. They would sing and dance all through our eras.

When they got to the jitter bug, it was all Vernon and I could do to keep from getting up and dancing with them. We spent a week in Branson, and we went to three different shows a day. It was so much fun. In all the shows, they would do a salute to the military, and it was touching to see all the older men and women stand when they played their song from their branch of service. We just loved it!

One time Jill found a special deal in Dahlonega, Georgia, at a lodge. It was a great package. All of the meals were included with our stay. We had adjoining rooms. Vernon and I had a big room with a hot tub.

After Vernon went to bed, Jill and I decided we would lounge in our hot tub. We got into our swim suits and into the hot tub. It was heaven! Our heaven turned around real soon when I could not get out of the tub. Jill and I tried everything. She hoisted, she wedged, she huffed, and she puffed trying to figure out how to get me out of that tub. We didn't know that Vernon was awake the whole time and was lying in the bed, trying to keep us from hearing him laugh. Well, our frustration continued.

Jill thought she was going to have to call the fire department to get me out of that tub. Finally, with much prayer, we accomplished our goal. I have not been too eager to get back in anymore hot tubs. I realized the power of prayer is what has carried me through my years. We still laugh about our evening to this day.

We really have had some wonderful times together. We have gone to Cypress Gardens, Grand Ole Opry, Myrtle Beach in South Carolina, and to Atlanta. In Atlanta, we saw the famous Rockettes and the magician, David Copperfield. We even went to Atlanta to see the Atlanta Braves play. Since Vernon loved golf so much, Dwain gave us tickets to go to The Masters in Augusta, Georgia. It was a sight to see.

As you can see, we haven't had much time to sit around. We always had something planned or someone in and out of our door.

Vernon and I enjoyed people so much that we decided we would become volunteers at the Bainbridge Hospital. We were called Red Cross Workers. We worked at different times during the week, twice a week. I worked in the front part of the hospital. I delivered mail and flowers to the patients in their rooms. We were allowed to talk with the patients if they wanted to talk. Vernon worked in the ICU. They would keep him busy with all kinds of errands.

One of the best things about working there is talking with different people. We really enjoyed it. The hospital would also give us a lunch plate for volunteering. I sure liked that because I didn't have to cook so much. We worked there for about eight years. They awarded us special throw blankets with the hospital logo and the year it was given. We received many compliments throughout the eight years.

Our family grew while Vernon and I were in the Shrine and working at the golf course. I now had a new hobby. It was our grand-children and great-grandchildren.

Chapter 47

Our Grandchildren and Great-Grandchildren

Travis, Jennifer, Shaw, and Cody Knight

My oldest son Dwain and his wife, Betty, blessed us with a cute red-headed granddaughter named Jennifer. She was born while Dwain was in the army, and they were stationed in Germany.

We didn't get to see her right away. It was hard to have a new granddaughter and not see her.

As Jennifer got older, they would visit us. She would always sleep beside me, and we would talk all night long. We had the best time! One time they were here, and Jennifer slipped up in my attic. Everyone always wanted to see what was in that attic! I really didn't know what all was up there myself.

I do know one thing that was up there—my love letters. I remember when Vernon was in the navy, on the USS *Enterprise* for three years during WWII. He wrote one hundred ninety-seven love letters. The box of love letters was in the attic. As a teenager, Jennifer wanted to read those letters.

When she came down from the attic, she said, "Granny, how did you read Papa's letter? I can't read his writing."

I said, "I know."

Jennifer is married now to Travis Knight. Travis works for Proctor and Gamble, and they have moved to Greensboro, North Carolina. Jennifer is a high school English teacher. Travis and Jennifer are just meant for each other.

They have added joy to our family with two sons. Shaw is eighteen and just graduated from high school. I was so lucky to attend my great-grandson's high school graduation at a ripe ole age of ninety-two! I was so proud of him, and I was so proud I could attend.

Cody is their second child. He is a very good football player, and I was also lucky enough to go and see him play in a game. I'm proud of all of them.

They now come and visit with me, and we have some good times. We have had a basketball goal in our yard for over fifty years, and the goal has outlived its time. It is hardly hanging, but the boys still go outside and shoot at the "ole standby."

Names left to right. Holland Shaw, Derek Shaw,
Brandi Shaw, Willa Kate Shaw, Lawren Love

My second son, Vernie, and his wife, Susan, blessed me with two grandchildren. Vernie and Susan's son's name is Derek Holland Shaw. It was such an honor to me for them to name Derek with my maiden name of Holland. I just loved that! Derek was such a sweet child. He really reminds me of Vernon. As he grew up, he was in and out of our house all the time. My favorite times with Derek were when he would come to see me, and we would sit around the table and talk. When I gave out of something to talk about, I would start telling him things that happen to me as a child. He seemed to like me doing that.

He was so patient, sweet, and listened to every word. This happened every time he came over. I'd start telling him a story again and that sweet smile would come on his face. When I think about it now, his sweet smile, I know he was thinking, *If she tells me that story one more time, I'm going to say nothing and let her tell it again.*

One time when Derek was visiting, Vernon, Jill, and Derek rode uptown to do something. Derek rode in the back seat, and he had found a pair of rabbit ears stuck behind one of the seats. He was just playing around with them. Vernon told Jill to pull into a gas station for gas. Derek spotted one of his buddies so he got out of the van to go over and speak to his friend, but he forgot he was wearing the rabbit's ears.

His buddy took one look at him and said, "Hey, man, what's with the ears?"

Well you hadn't seen anyone grab something off their head so fast! I can only imagine what he told the guy. Vernon and Jill saw it, and Vernon started laughing. He laughed so hard, the entire van was shaking.

When they came home, Vernon and Jill were still laughing. It has been one the funniest stories about Derek his whole life. We kidded him for years and told him that when he graduated from school, we would all be in the audience with rabbit ears! Derek has been a great sport about this! He was so patient and good to me.

Derek is married to a very sweet girl, Brandy. They live in Whigham, Georgia. Derek is an x-ray technician at Archibald Memorial Hospital in Thomasville, Georgia. Brandy works in health care in Thomasville. Brandy has a daughter from a previous marriage. Her name is Lawren. Derek and Brandy had another little girl on July 18, 2014. I was thrilled to know they were naming her Derek's middle name and my maiden name. Her name is Holland Reese Shaw! On May 14, 2016, Derek and Brandy blessed our family with a third little girl. Her name is Willa Kate Shaw. I enjoy it when they visit me.

The names left to right. Sarah Shaw, Bert Nix, Rebecca
Nix, Bella Nix, Payten Nix, Anna Lisa Nix

Vernie and Susan had a daughter named Susan Rebecca Shaw.
She was named after her mother. Rebecca was the prettiest little girl I
think I've ever seen. She had a head full of blond curls and was such
a happy-go-lucky child. She looked like Shirley Temple.

When she was four years old, Vernie and Susan entered her in
a beauty contest sponsored by the Pilot Club. When she walked out
on stage, she got everyone's attention. She won first place in her age
group. When Rebecca was growing up, she would come and visit me
real often. One day, she came and I was starting to make my mayhaw jelly, and she wanted to help me. I told her she was just in time
to help me. When it came time to fill the jars with jelly, I would let
Rebecca pour it. I would tell her when the jar was full. I would let
her tighten the lids down on the jars real tight, and we had jelly. She
was so proud of herself! Rebecca and I cooked together many times.
I was trying to teach her some of my ways.

Rebecca was very good in sports, and it thrilled me to go and watch Rebecca play. She played basketball and softball. She was great in both! She was so talented in softball that she ended up with a scholarship to play softball at Middle Georgia College. When Rebecca came back to Bainbridge, she blessed me with a little great-granddaughter named after me. Her name is Sarah Elizabeth Shaw. She has been a shining light for all of us. She is smart and talented. She likes to cook for me. I'm so very proud of Rebecca. She is married to Bert Nix. They live in Climax, Georgia. Rebecca is a registered nurse at Archibald Memorial Hospital in Thomasville, Georgia. Bert is an industrial mechanic for BASF. Bert has two daughters from a previous marriage. One daughter's name is Payten. Payten is so sweet to me. She is really a pretty girl. His second daughter's name is Anna Lisa. She has long beautiful blonde hair and entertains me with her dances and art skills. On August 11, 2016, Bert and Rebecca had a fourth little girl. Her name is Bella Sky Nix. Bert, Rebecca, and the girls have really been a blessing to me. They are now one big, happy family!

My Favorite Flower Is the Rose

When I think of all my children and grandchildren, I think of them as my rose bush.

My roses just keep on growing with every grandchild and great-grandchild.

I am truly blessed!

Brookie

My youngest daughter, Tammy, and her husband, Tommy, gave me my brunette granddaughter. Her name is Brookie Charlene Connell. Brookie was named after Tommy's mother, Charlene.

Now, I have a redheaded granddaughter, a blonde granddaughter, and a beautiful brunette granddaughter. Brookie was a doll. We spent a lot of time home together. She would spend the night, and we would play, cook, sew, and read. She was my shadow.

One day, she asked me if I had anything to eat. I looked in the refrigerator and found some jello in a dish. I gave it to her. She looked at it and didn't say anything.

She looked at the jello and said, "Granny, how do you make jello with green fuzz on it?"

I looked at it and, sure enough, it had green fuzz on it. I quickly said, "Don't eat that."

I took it and threw it away. I found something to make a sandwich out of and that was okay with her. I got the bread and smeared peanut butter and jelly on it. I cut the crust off my bread and cut it down the middle so I could hold it better.

I gave Brookie her part, and she said, "Granny, why do you cut the crust off the sides of the bread?"

I said, "Because I like it better that way." Well, I found out from Brookie years later that she will not eat a sandwich any other way.

One day, Brookie wanted to play basketball. She loved to go out and try to hit the goal. She would want Granny to go with her and show her how. I played basketball when I was in school and when I shot a goal, I would aim for the backboard and the ball would go in the basket every time. Nowadays when I watch basketball on television, they shoot for the basket. Brookie was pretty good at basketball, but she did not end up playing. She joined the band and played flute until she won Drum Major for the Bainbridge high school band.

Brookie went to Georgia Southern College and majored in elementary education. She taught in Atlanta, Georgia, for years. She met a great friend named Lisa Parker. Lisa and Brookie added some adventures in their lives and moved to Costa Rica. They liked it so well there that they have started a business.

They live in a town close to the beach. It is a tourist location. They are catering to the tourist population with organically made popsicles. I'm very proud of Brookie, and if I know my Brookie she will be a very prosperous business owner. She visits with me about once a year, and I love it when she is home. Brookie continues using her teaching skills by teaching online. I'm proud of that too.

The names left to right Grady Connell,
Gracie Jillian Connell, Kasey Connell

Tammy and Tommy also have a son. His name is Grady Thomas Connell Jr., named after his daddy. We call him Thomas. The name Grady came from his great-grandfather. The name Thomas came from his daddy, his daddy's grandfather and his Papa Vernon. It sure did make Vernon happy. We were so happy to have our fifth grandchild.

Thomas spent a lot of time with us as well. He was very independent as a little boy. He was always turning and pushing buttons and checking out everything. I always knew where Thomas had been in the house because my knobs had been turned around. He was always tinkering. When he was thirteen, he built a computer for his Aunt Jill. He was always very smart and still is to this day!

As Thomas grew older, I could depend on him to fix anything in my house. He would change batteries, reset my remotes, and reset my VCR every time I messed it up. He was always helping me in one way or another. Thomas and I would get in the kitchen together, and we would bake us some oatmeal cookies. He loved those cookies so we made them quite a bit.

One time when Thomas was here, we went to the grocery store. When I went to check out, I used a credit card.

When we were walking to the car, Thomas said, "Granny, you didn't give them any money."

I told him about the plastic credit card. He was so amazed.

He said, "I'm going to tell Mama that she needs to get one of those cards, and she won't need money." I have laughed about that over the years!

Thomas is very independent. He would do what he needed to do on his own. He was great with his hands, whether it was playing a drum or fixing a car. He is quite talented. Thomas followed in Brookie's footsteps. He played the drums in the band. He also tried his luck at playing the fiddle. The music gene has carried on throughout our family.

Thomas actually came and lived with me for a while. I enjoyed him being with me.

Today, Thomas is the owner of Tip Top Auto Shop in Tallahassee, Florida. He is a great car mechanic. I'm so proud of his talent. Kasey is a secretary for the Attorney General of Florida in Tallahassee, Florida.

Thomas and Kasey married on October 31, 2015. Kasey is so sweet and caring. She fits right in with our family. Thomas and Kasey gave me the most beautiful bracelet for Christmas. I will cherish it always! Thomas and Kasey had a baby girl, Gracie Jillian Connell, born on November 18th, 2016. I'm so proud of Thomas.

Many times we would have all the grandchildren over for special times. Halloween was one of those times. We would dress the grandchildren up for trick-or-treat, and many times I actually made Brookie and Thomas a costume. I would also make a costume for Vernon and me to wear. Sometimes we would go trick-or-treating with them. Sometimes we just gave out candy at the door. It was a tradition for us to trick-or-treat. Then, everyone would end up back at home to have a pizza party. I would order the pizza while they were out trick-or-treating. Now that the grandkids are grown, we still carry on our Halloween tradition with their children. It has always been a fun time for the family.

Easter Sunday was another very special time for us. On Saturday, we boiled about two dozen eggs. I would take the kids' crayons and decorate them. I always saved some for them to decorate. We would go to church on Easter Sunday morning. Vernon would hide the eggs. The kids would come, and the girls would be dressed in their pretty Easter clothes with their little Easter baskets. The eggs were so pretty. All of them were different. We would have a prize egg, and the one who found it would win a candy bar. Derek would help the little ones find the eggs. He also often found that prize egg. After we found the eggs, we would all go inside and crack the boiled eggs to eat. They took home the eggs that were not eaten. It was so much fun!

Derek, Brookie, Rebecca, and Thomas

Once when Brookie and Rebecca were visiting with us, they would have themselves a good ole time. They wanted to put on my dresses, hats, and sandals. They would dress up and then parade to show me. One day, they really surprised me. They dressed up in my clothes and put oranges under the top in the spot for their boobs. It was really a sight, and all of us laughed and laughed! I told them I thought that was enough for one day. I actually loved having the kids in and out all the time. It was great!

I'm writing this in July 2015, and as of today, I have five grand-children and seven great-grandchildren. I hope and pray my rose garden will continue to grow. I look forward to enjoying any new rose buds that may come along. My roses are blooming, and as you can see they are all *very* special to me!

Chapter 48

The Loss of the Love of My Life

I told you that Vernon worked for about eight years at the Pines Golf Course. When the golf course decided to make some changes, they told Vernon they didn't need him anymore. In my heart, I feel like this hurt Vernon. He seemed to lose interest in life. You know at Vernon's heaviest, he weighed 250 pounds. He seemed to begin to lose weight. He developed a more serious disease, chronic obstructive pulmonary disease (COPD).

In 2003, Vernon fell and broke his hip. He ended up in the Bainbridge Hospital for over a month. Jill had just retired from teaching in Valdosta, so she came and stayed in the hospital with him. After he came home from the hospital, he just didn't seem to bounce back. I would ask him if he was hurting.

He would say, "I don't hurt. I just don't feel good."

I was at a loss to help him. I worked and worked with him trying to get him to bounce back. He seemed content to just sit and watch television. When the kids would come over, he still seemed content to sit and watch his television.

Vernon loved sports and he would watch the Braves and he would watch the Masters. He loved his Georgia Bulldogs. When he started losing interest in his sports, I was truly at a loss. This day-in and day-out routine was wearing me down.

Jill took notice, and she closed her home in Valdosta and came to Bainbridge to help me with Vernon. He was continually losing weight. All his favorite dishes did not phase him. He was steadily going downhill.

Jill and I tried a little trip to see if that would help. We took him to the Naval Museum in Pensacola, Florida. The museum worked. Vernon really seemed to bounce back. He saw a replica of his ship, and he stood up from of his wheelchair and started talking about his service on the ship USS *Enterprise*. When we looked up, Vernon had a crowd surrounding him. When he finished talking, everyone was clapping. I will never forget that.

When we returned home, Vernon seemed to be doing a little better. We had been taking him for check-ups at the Veteran's Hospital in Tallahassee, Florida. He was meeting with a doctor who diagnosed him with dementia. I had noticed a few memory problems on and off for a while. It was very hard to believe it. Some days he was okay, but other days, it would really show up. Jill and I would try and keep him going. We would go out to eat. We would also try to go out to the movies. We would go to the mall and walk. We just tried our best to interest him in life again. No matter what we did, he was really going downhill fast.

On November 21, 2007, right before Thanksgiving, I went into his room to feed him some oatmeal. Vernon looked at me and said, "I just had lunch with my Master." Do you know that was the last thing I ever heard Vernon say? He was eighty-six years old.

Brookie was home from teaching school for Thanksgiving. Jill and Brookie went in to check on Vernon. Brookie said, "Aunt Jill, Papa's not moving."

Vernon truly had lunch with his Master. He knew something that I did not realize. Brookie and Jill came into my room. I was visiting with two of his Shrine friends who had come to visit. They asked the men to leave, and they told me. I screamed and ran to him. I was so sad that I wasn't by his side when it happened. He closed his eyes and went to sleep.

I can say this to you truthfully. The love of my life of sixty-two years passed away very peacefully and part of me passed away with him. We called all the family in. Instead of coming for Thanksgiving, everyone was coming home to honor their dad at his "going home" service. Vernon had a Masonic funeral and military honors. They presented me with the American flag. Dwain had the flag placed in a shadowbox frame to preserve it.

I was lost. I was numb and grieving. It was a long time before I could even think. I knew it would happen one day, but I just wasn't prepared to continue living without him.

Chapter 49

Life Goes On

I was just going through the motions of life for about a year.

I would eat, sleep, breathe, and rest. That was about it. It took a while to start living again. I did as I've always done, which was to rely on the power of prayer. I was so exhausted from taking care of Vernon and everything pertaining to our life that I had a really hard time getting back to living. Jill stayed here with me and helped me get back on my feet.

Slowly and surely, things got a little bit easier. I was doing okay except I was beginning to have trouble with my balance. I would be walking along just fine, and suddenly, I would start falling backwards. The only explanation I could get from anyone was I had developed neuropathy in my feet because of diabetes. This would make my balance very unsteady. I began falling here and there. Luckily, I have enough padding on my hips to keep me from breaking anything.

One night, at about twelve, I thought I needed to take the trashcan out to the curb because they were coming to pick up the trash the next morning. I had my pajamas on and I didn't think anyone would see me. I was wrong.

The big lid on that trash can hit me on the head, and I fell flat on the ground. Luckily, there was a little grass on the ground. Oh boy, I was in a pickle! When I fell, I couldn't get up by myself. Eventually, I sat up and wiggled myself over to the curb. I started waving at every car that went by. I know people were thinking, *What in the world is that person doing sitting out here waving at people at this time of night?*

No one stopped. I had no way of getting up. I just started praying and a young man that lived close to us saw me.

He stopped and got out and said, "Ms. Shaw, do you need some help?"

I was so relieved! I said, "Yes, I sure do!"

He helped get me up and helped me back in the house.

Thank goodness for him. I thanked him. I know in my heart who sent that young man my way. I do believe that was the very last time any of the Shaws carried trash to the curb. The city takes care of that chore for me.

Even though Jill was staying with me, she was still teaching part-time in Thomasville. She would make sure I was okay and off she would go to work. One of the times she was gone, I was by myself. Vernie and Susan were out of town too. I went into the kitchen into the pantry to find me something to eat. I was inside the freezer part of the refrigerator, and the door knocked me off balance. I was holding on, but I knew I was going down. I just eased myself to the floor.

I wasn't hurt, but I was stuck on the ground again. I had a phone and my alarm button on me, but the batteries were dead in both. I was in a mess now. I scooted over to the step that went from the pantry to the dining room. I had no idea how I was going to make it up the step.

I laid out flat over the step and rolled on my stomach to get myself out of the pantry. Luckily my reacher was nearby, so I grabbed it and reached for the phone.

I called Derek. There was no answer so I called Rebecca. I told her I had fallen, and I needed help. Rebecca lived in Climax, Georgia, so I knew it would take her a little while to get here. I took my reacher and got as many cushions out of the chairs as I could. I tried to make myself comfortable. I had been reading a book, and it was on the table so I got it. I got the book and just sat back on the floor, reading my book.

In the meantime, Rebecca got a hold of Derek, and he had to go to Lucy's house who has been our helper for many years. She had a key to get in. It wasn't fifteen minutes later that the entire family walked in. Bert, Rebecca, the three girls, and Derek walked in. I could hear Rebecca telling the girls that Mimi (that's what they called me) had fallen and they needed to sit in the back and not say a word. When Rebecca came around the corner, she saw me sitting and reading. I just waved at her. We busted out laughing. I knew I was okay, but she did not. They readily came to my rescue, and I will never forget that day. I'm sure Rebecca, the family, and Derek will not either.

The falls continued on and off, and I've lost count of the actual number of falls I've had. I know it is at least twenty-five. I haven't been quite so lucky all the time. The day after my eighty-fifth birthday, I took a bad fall and fractured my hip. Of course out to Bainbridge Hospital I went. I was there quite a while. Jill has worked hard to encourage me to get better.

She told me as soon as I got better, she would take me on a trip. My only sister had moved to Oklahoma to be near her son and her grandchildren. Jill told me we would go and see Aunt Lottie when I was better.

I did get better and Jill took me on a two-week trip. We started our trip and headed to Biloxi, Mississippi. I had not ever been to a casino. We went and Jill had a hard time getting me to leave and go to bed. I really enjoyed it.

Our trip continued to Little Rock, Arkansas. We stayed in Little Rock. We went to check in the hotel and no one wanted to help us. They were glued to the television for the American Idol Finale, and one of the boys up to win was from that town. I didn't know if we would get in a room or not. Come to find out the local boy, Kris Allen, did win, and most everyone in the town was celebrating at the football field. It was really neat to us.

The next day, we headed toward Oklahoma. Neither one of us thought we would ever get there! It seemed the closer we got, the farther away it was.

We did make it, and I was so glad to see Lottie. Her son, Myron, and his wife, Terri, had planned some activities for us while we were visiting. We ended up at the Oklahoma State Aquarium. Myron was pushing Lottie around the aquarium in a wheelchair, and Jill was pushing me around in a wheelchair. We were a sight, I'm sure! Our visit with Lottie was great! It was short, but it was so special!

I did not know at the time we left that it would be the last time I got to see my sister. Lottie died of a stroke not more than a year after we were there. Her son brought her back to Cuthbert, Georgia, to be buried next to G.H., her husband. Jill and I will go visit Lottie and G.H.'s grave and make sure that she knows she is missed. Lottie and I were so close throughout our life, and I miss her every day.

When Jill and I left Oklahoma, we found our way back to Branson, Missouri. We were not there twenty minutes before we went back to some of our favorite music shows. We enjoyed it there and stayed several days. It was great, but we sure did miss Vernon being with us.

In my spare time as I'm sitting around at home, I'm enjoying making scrapbooks for all my children and grandchildren. I have made almost all of them a memory book. I'm working on another one right now that I want to give to Thomas at Christmas. It will be good because his birthday is in December. He will like that present from me.

I do stay very busy, and I like it that way. Every time I get a new book, I just want to stay up all night and read, read, read! You know what? Sometimes I do! Retirement has been great!

I have three brothers still living. Two of my brothers live in Fernandina, and my other brother lives in Brewton, Alabama. My baby brother Burnell Holland is still working in Fernandina. He owns an automobile repair shop.

My brothers Nerle Holland and James Holland, are retired, so they will come to Bainbridge and meet each other here. Their wives join them. We all gather around my dining room table and talk about the good ole days and anything else that comes up. We will go to lunch together and spend a little more time together before they leave and head back to their homes. Those visits have really been a blessing! We have maintained our closeness even if it is only for one day. We get together when everyone is feeling okay, and its usually two or three times a year. I love my brothers and their families. They have treated me very special.

I told you Jill works part-time, and she has a home in Valdosta. When she works and goes to her home, sometimes, my daughter

Tammy helps me. Tammy is a retired nurse, and she continues her love of nursing with me. Her husband, Tommy, has been so supportive in helping take care of me too. I sure have kept Jill and Tammy hopping. It seems we weather one obstacle and something else will pop up. I have the most wonderful children! They have *all* taken care of me in one way or another. I have two of the most wonderful daughters that share the direct care of me. I feel very lucky to have them. They have both told me at different times they are the lucky ones. You know, that's a good feeling!

Lucy Carter is also a very special person in my life. She has been with me through thick and thin for over forty years. She has always been a big part of the Shaw Family. I love and appreciate her dedication to our family.

When I turned ninety years old in 2013, my children went all out. They honored me with a birthday party at the Kirbo Center. We had about fifty people at this party. The children and grandchildren spoke about their special time that they have shared with me. It was so touching. I was so proud.

I got to entertain the crowd by playing my harmonica. My favorite song is "The Rose" so I played it that night. You know that was the first time many of my family members ever heard me play?

I loved playing and I enjoyed sharing it that night. Not only did the children give me a big party, but they also gave me a trip to Niagara Falls.

Niagara Falls

Jill and I met her friend Joan in Atlanta, and we flew to Buffalo, New York. We rented a car and drove into Niagara Falls. It was a sight to behold. I had seen it once before when we went to Toronto, Canada, with the Shriners, but we were only there for one day. Jill, Joan, and I were there for several days. We stayed at Embassy Suites on the 15th floor, and our room overlooked the falls.

Joan and I are on the lower level of this boat with our rain gear on. It was beautiful. At night, they would shine different color lights on the falls. It was really unbelievable. I've never seen a place so beautiful. The entire town had beautiful flowers everywhere. We toured all over Niagara Falls! It was the best birthday present!

Joan and I even rode the *Maid-of-the-Mist* boat under the falls. It was great to see the falls from below. She was so sweet to go with us and help me so much. She is like a daughter to me. The three of us had the best time.

When we got ourselves back to Bainbridge, Georgia, I had to rest for a couple of months. It was such a great birthday year! Actually, I'm really looking forward to my next big birthday surprise!

I've enjoyed my times traveling, and I've enjoyed my times at home. I just wish my body would let me do all the things I still want to do. I keep trying.

Everything was going pretty well until I had a very nasty fall. I fractured the vertebrae in my back and ended up back at the Bainbridge Hospital. I ended up staying for three weeks. I had complications with the fall which really slowed my recovery down. I have spent the last year trying to get back to good health.

Today about one entire year later, I am feeling better. I realize God is just not through with me. He knows I am a good worker. I actually filled one hundred Easter eggs with candy for my church, and I also filled one hundred bottles with peppermint for Vacation Bible School. I enjoy doing what I can to help wherever I can.

I enjoy my family times and all our holiday times. Our Christmases have always been special. Everyone comes and we celebrate Christmas all together. We still give Christmas presents to every single person. We sit around in a circle, and each person opens their present so everyone can see what they got. We have always had that circle of love in our family, and I hope we always will.

Vernon always said, "Now you make sure everybody has something to open."

We also make it special every year with candy. There is always a small plate of candy right by everyone while we take our time opening presents.

Oh, those special traditions!

Chapter 50

The Golden Years

I can certainly say I have had the best life can give. When I started my book, I was thinking of all the things I've had the chance to do. I thought I'd like for children and adults to know the things we had when I was growing up. They would never believe all the things that we did.

I'm ninety-two years old, and I have shared my life with you in all fifty chapters! I would like you to know I'm enjoying my life. I'm living in my own home. I can walk. I still pay my own bills. I thank God every day for letting me live to my age. I am in love with God's beautiful world. It has been home to me.

I cannot say enough about how proud I am of my children, my grandchildren, and my great-grandchildren. I only hope all of their lives will be as blessed as mine has been.

I pray my roses will continue to grow and grow.

I always wondered how and why I ended up in Bainbridge, Georgia. It came to me when I found out that there were many turpentine stills in and around Bainbridge in the good ole days. I feel like I've come home. God led me here just as He has guided every step I've ever taken.

My Favorite Bible Verse:

This is the day that the Lord has made.
Let us rejoice and be glad in it.
I've strived to live this verse all my life.

As I face the future, I have this belief that *this* turpentine girl's *best* is yet to be!

Appendix

My Rose Garden

Throughout

The Years

My Family

The Children of William Dodson Kilgore
And Sarah Dryden Kilgore
(My Aunts and Uncles)

Back Row: George, Gordon, Elbert

Front Row: Rosa Lee, Mary, Mae Bell

My Parents

Mae Bell, Vivian Holland

Vernon's Parents (My Dear In-Laws)

Bessie McCard Shaw, James Livingston Shaw

My Siblings and Their Spouses

My brother and his wife
Louwana and Wilford Holland

My sister and her husband
Lottie and G.H. Ford

My brother and his wife
James and June Holland

My Siblings and Their Spouses

My brother and his wife
Grace Earl and Nerle Holland

My brother and his wife
Burnelle and Betty Jo Holland.

My Siblings and My Mama

Back Row: James, Wilford, Burnelle, Nerle
Front Row: Lottie, Mae Bell, and Evelyn

Our Children and Their Families

My Oldest Son and His Wife
Dwain, Evelyn, and Leilani

My Oldest Daughter and Me
Jill and Me

My Youngest Son and His Family

Back Row: Brandy, Derek, Vernie, and Bert
Middle Row: Susan, Rebecca, and Payten
Front Row: Sarah, Mimi, and Anna Lisa
Not Pictured: Lawren

My Youngest Daughter and Her Family
Brookie, Thomas, Me, Tommy, and Tammy

Tammy. Dwain, Me, Vernie, and Jill

Me and Vernon

My Rose Garden
Throughout the Years

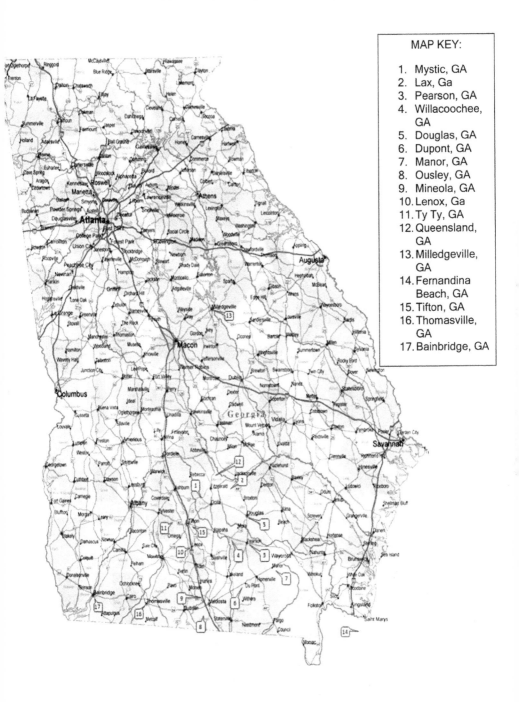

MAP KEY:

1. Mystic, GA
2. Lax, Ga
3. Pearson, GA
4. Willacoochee, GA
5. Douglas, GA
6. Dupont, GA
7. Manor, GA
8. Ousley, GA
9. Mineola, GA
10. Lenox, Ga
11. Ty Ty, GA
12. Queensland, GA
13. Milledgeville, GA
14. Fernandina Beach, GA
15. Tifton, GA
16. Thomasville, GA
17. Bainbridge, GA

About the Author

Evelyn Shaw lives in her home in Bainbridge, Georgia with her daughter, Jill. She is 94 years old as of February 4th, 2017 and is enjoying life. Her passions include reading, scrapbooking, and spending time with her growing family.

She sincerely hopes this book will be an inspiration to all the readers.

Sarah Evelyn Holland Shaw entered her
heavenly home on July 20th, 2017.
Her family is so proud of this gift she has given to us.

God Bless You, Mama.

Lightning Source UK Ltd.
Milton Keynes UK
UKHW011310260220
359369UK00002B/451